Core Maths In a Week

Level 3 Certificate Mathematical Studies

Jim Clayden and Simon Moroney

AQA

CONTENTS

Types of Data

LEARNING OBJECTIVES

You need to be able to appreciate the difference between qualitative and quantitative data.

Data is information. It can be split into two main types:

- **Quantitative** – data obtained by counting or measuring.
- **Qualitative** – data that describes a quality or non-numerical aspect of an item or good.

Quantitative Data

Quantitative data comes in two forms: **discrete** and **continuous**.

Discrete data has exact values. For example, you can count the number of:

- children in a household
- pets owned by a family
- light bulbs (or any other item) produced by a factory per hour.

Shoe size is also an example of discrete data, e.g. 6, $6\frac{1}{2}$, 7, $7\frac{1}{2}$, etc. There are no values between these set sizes.

Continuous data can take any value in a given range. For example, you can measure:

- time
- distance
- width, height and length
- weight and mass.

Qualitative Data

Some things can only be described (they cannot be counted or measured). For example:

- the colour of something (e.g. red, blue, green)
- the make or type of an item (e.g. a car might be a BMW or Ford, a hatchback or convertible)
- the type or breed of a pet.

Be careful of grey areas, such as how confidence, preference or likelihood are assessed:

- If something is likely/unlikely, the data is qualitative.
- If there is a 95% chance of something happening, the data is quantitative.
- Sometimes numbers are selected by making a judgement rather than a measurement, so the data is actually qualitative, e.g. a Likert scale from 0 to 5 where 0 is 'totally disagree' and 5 is 'totally agree'.

SUMMARY

- **Data is either qualitative (descriptive) or quantitative (countable/measurable).**
- **If data is quantitative, it is either discrete (exact values) or continuous (can take any value).**

1. Decide whether each of the following is **quantitative** or **qualitative**.

   If it is qualitative, state whether the data is **discrete** or **continuous**.

   a) Model or manufacturer of car

   b) Length of a piece of string

   c) Number of pets in a household

   d) Favourite political party

   e) The likelihood that you will pass this Level 3 course

   f) Your age

2. Look at the photograph on the right.

   When planning the building, the architect had to produce lots of data about its dimensions and the materials needed.

   a) Name **three** variables that an architect could record that are qualitative.

   b) Name **three** variables that an architect could record that are quantitative. Include examples of both continuous and discrete data.

PRACTICE QUESTION

1. In a census, the government asks for information about the number of occupants in each house or home on that day.

   What type of data is collected by the government?
   Tick all boxes that apply.   **[2 marks]**

   quantitative   qualitative   discrete   continuous

   ☐   ☐   ☐   ☐

Collecting and Sampling Data

Primary data is data you have collected yourself, e.g. using your own questionnaires or surveys.

Secondary data comes from other sources, e.g. the Internet. The data gathering work has already been done. However, filtering may be required.

If you use secondary data, you must credit the source.

Data can be collected via:
- observations, e.g. counting or observing aspects of cars in a car park
- interviews, e.g. asking job applicants a number of set questions and recording the answers
- questionnaires, e.g. a set of written questions (with a choice of answers) about holiday preferences that individuals are asked to complete as part of a survey commissioned by a travel company
- experiments, e.g. a controlled experiment to find the temperature at which a set amount of instant coffee dissolves quickest in water
- tests, e.g. factory tests on the longevity of a light bulb
- other methods.

Sometimes one data variable may be compared with another (as in scientific experiments).

Where appropriate, you need to be able to identify:
- the **independent (explanatory) variable**, e.g. the temperature
- the **dependent (responsive) variable**, e.g. the number of ice creams sold.

Generally speaking the number of ice creams sold is dependent on the temperature. However, be careful of **spurious** correlations, where there is little or no connection between the two data sets.

It is also necessary to be aware of **bias** (a leaning towards a favourite, such as a football team or political candidate). Removing bias will improve the accuracy of the data collected.

Methods

Ideally, when collecting data, the whole **population** of a data set should be considered. However, in practice, this can be very time-consuming and expensive.

A **census** asks for all the members of a population (e.g. of a country or club) to give feedback and provides an understanding of trends within the whole population. The British Government carries out a census every 10 years to gain a complete picture of the nation and help with future policies and planning.

Sampling (taking only a portion of the population) is often used to reduce expense and time. However, it is important to make the sample as representative as possible. The table describes some of the methods that can be used to do this.

Type of Sample	Definition	Conditions or Properties	Advantages	Disadvantages
Random	Every member of the population (the sampling frame) has the same chance of being selected, usually via the use of a random number generator or table or an equivalent computer program.	Members or items are similar.	No bias	Time-consuming
Cluster	Used when there are obvious different (heterogeneous) groups within a population. Random sampling is then applied to the groups. Often used in market research.	Distinctive groups or types within a population are necessary.	Usually cheaper than random and able to show regional variations.	Not a true random sample; can be biased.
Stratified	Each stratum (layer) of a population is represented in proportion to the size of that stratum. Random sampling occurs within the strata.	Members are similar with identifiable groups or layers, e.g. year groups in a school.	Proportionally representative; can highlight trends in each layer.	Time-consuming
Quota	A given number of members from sections (or layers) are chosen by the interviewer. Randomness is not necessary.	Identifiable groups necessary, e.g. gender, age, race, etc.	Easy to capture for most sections.	Subjective; not truly random; bias is likely.

SUMMARY

- Collected data is either:
  - ○ primary – collected first-hand
  - ○ secondary – collected by someone else.
- Sampling is choosing part or some of the population.
- The main sampling methods are:
  - ○ random – all items have same chance of selection
  - ○ cluster – a random sample is taken from each distinctive group
  - ○ stratified – a random sample is taken each stratum (layer); the size of the samples are proportional to the size of the strata
  - ○ quota – a set quantity is chosen from each section at will.
- The advantages of sampling are usually about saving time, saving money or fairness.

DAY 1

QUICK TEST

1. State whether each of the following is **primary** or **secondary** data:
   a) A survey of the colours and types of car in a staff car park.
   b) Downloading house price data from the Land Registry website.
   c) Asking people on a high street the name of their favourite football team.
   d) An energy company accepting the electricity meter reading from a customer.
2. A journalist wants to write a story on the effectiveness of a drug on patients of different ages.
   a) Should they use primary or secondary data? Explain your answer.
   b) What type of sample could be used and why?

PRACTICE QUESTIONS

1. The table below shows different sections of 300 eligible voters from a village.

Age Group	18–25	26–50	51+
Male	52	29	63
Female	48	30	78
Total	100	59	141

A political pollster wants to find out the opinions of a sample of 30 voters.
They choose five males and five females from each age group.

a) Explain why this is **not** a representative sample. [2 marks]

b) Give a full description of a better sampling method the pollster could use. Include the number of voters that should be chosen from each category. [4 marks]

2. There are 20 members in a local cooperative.

Age Group	Number of Members
18–35	7
36–50	9
51–65	4

A sample size of six is to be chosen.

a) Describe how a cluster sample might be chosen. [2 marks]

b) Using this table of random numbers, show how a sample of six could be chosen for:

Random Number		
51	8	69
88	54	85
37	49	93
91	93	93
22	79	39
1	42	84
100	22	86
33	78	18
78	15	2
56	1	34
19	89	2
73	89	87
19	38	23
10	72	37
92	69	59

i) a random sample [3 marks]

ii) a stratified sample. [4 marks]

3. A company wishes to discuss issues with a sample of its employees.

Area	Number of Employees
Executive	12
Administrators	20
Supervisors	10
IT Support	6
Manual Staff	102
All	**150**

a) Calculate how many employees from each area should be involved in a stratified sample of 21 employees. [4 marks]

b) A different stratified sample contains 10 manual staff.

Work out the size of the total sample. [2 marks]

Representing Data Numerically

You need to be able to:

● identify and calculate the different averages, percentiles, quartiles, interquartile range and standard deviation

● interpret these numerical measures and use them to reach conclusions.

Measures of Central Tendency and Spread

Measure	Definition	Advantages	Disadvantages
Mean ($\bar{x}$)	All the values are added together and divided by the total number of values.	All the data items are used. **Example Data Set:** **2, 20, 22, 23, 23** $$\text{Mean} = \frac{(2 + 20 + 22 + 23 + 23)}{5}$$ $$= 18$$	Distorted by extreme values. In the example data set, 2 is an extreme and makes the mean questionable, i.e. possibly unrepresentative.
Mode	The most common/ frequently occurring item or class interval.	Good for qualitative data. No calculations are needed to identify the mode value.	Could be unrepresentative if a value is only repeated a few times or if two or three modes occur. In the example data set, 23 is the mode and questionable.
Median (Q_2)	The centre value (50th percentile) when the values are arranged in numerical order. If there is an even number of values in the data set, find the midpoint of the two central values.	Not affected by extreme values. For the example data set: Median = 22	Limited mathematical influence as it is stagnant (does not move).
Range	The difference between the largest and smallest value in the data set.	Gives the largest spread of the data. For the example data set: Range = 23 − 2 = 21	Extreme values may not represent the majority picture of the data. In the example data set, ignoring extremes gives a range of 23 − 20 = 3

Upper Quartile (Q_3)	The 75th percentile, i.e. the value $\frac{3}{4}$ or 75% of the way through the data set.	Not affected by extreme values.	Not all values are considered.
Lower Quartile (Q_1)	The 25th percentile, i.e. the value $\frac{1}{4}$ or 25% of the way through the data set.		In the example data set, the extreme of 2 is included when finding Q_1 and Q_3.
Interquartile Range (IQR)	The difference between the upper quartile (Q_3) and the lower quartile (Q_1).	Gives the spread for the middle 50% of the data set. Reduces effect of extremes. See below for examples.	Ignores half of the data.

Example

Here is a discrete data set:

2, 4, 7, 10, 12, 12, 17, 23

Mean $= \dfrac{(2 + 4 + 7 + 10 + 12 + 12 + 17 + 23)}{8} = \dfrac{87}{8}$

$\quad\quad = 10.875$

Mode $= 12$

Median $= \dfrac{(10 + 12)}{8} = 11$

Range $= 23 - 2 = 21$

$Q_3 \quad = \dfrac{(12 + 17)}{2} = 14.5$

$Q1 \quad = \dfrac{(4 + 7)}{2} = 5.5$

IQR $\quad = 14.5 - 5.5 = 9$

For an example using grouped data, see Representing Data in Diagrams (pages 14–17).

Standard Deviation (SD)

Standard deviation is effectively a 'mean distance' from the mean of the data set.

As a measure, standard deviation can compare how different data sets are spread out.

It is usually denoted by the Greek letter σ (sigma) and can be calculated using either of the following two methods.

Method 1

$\sigma = \sqrt{\dfrac{\Sigma(x - \bar{x})^2}{n - 1}}$ or $\sigma = \sqrt{\dfrac{\Sigma f(x - \bar{x})^2}{\Sigma f}}$ (discrete frequency distribution)

where Σ means 'the sum of', x is a data point, $\bar{x}$ is the sample mean and n is the sample size.

Method 2

$\sigma = \sqrt{\dfrac{\Sigma x^2}{n - 1} - \bar{x}^2}$ or $\sigma = \sqrt{\dfrac{\Sigma f x^2}{\Sigma f} - \bar{x}^2}$ (discrete frequency distribution)

where x is a data point, $\bar{x}$ is the sample mean and n is the sample size.

How the formulae are derived is not tested in this course. However, you do need to appreciate what the scores imply in the context of a problem.

For example, the mean number of goals per game in a football league is 2.59, with a standard deviation of 1.63.

This implies that most goals (within one standard either side) will be between 0.96 and 4.22.

Of course, none of these scores are actually possible in a game – it generally suggests scores of 1 to 4 goals per game. (You will learn later that if the goals are normally distributed, this should account for around 65% of games – see pages 56–59.)

It would also be impossible to score two standard deviations below the mean, as this would give a value of –0.67 (In reality, this would be zero goals scored.)

Example

Calculate the standard deviation for the following discrete data set:

2, 4, 5, 5, 6, 8, 9, 9, 10, 11

First calculate the mean:

$$\bar{x} = \frac{(2 + 4 + 5 + 5 + 6 + 8 + 9 + 9 + 10 + 11)}{10} = 6.9$$

Then substitute into one of the formulae to calculate the standard deviation:

Using Method 1

$$\sigma = (2 - 6.9)^2 + (4-6.9)^2 + \ldots + (11-6.9)^2$$

$$\sigma = \sqrt{\frac{\Sigma(x - \bar{x})^2}{n - 1}}$$

$$\sigma = \sqrt{\frac{(2 - 6.9)^2 + (4 - 6.9)^2 + \ldots + (11 - 6.9)^2}{10 - 1}}$$

$$\sigma = 2.923$$

Using Method 2

$$\sigma = \sqrt{\frac{\Sigma x^2}{n - 1} - \bar{x}^2}$$

$$\sigma = \sqrt{\frac{2^2 + 4^2 + \ldots + 10^2 + 11^2}{10 - 1} - 6.9^2}$$

$$\sigma = 2.923$$

All this can be calculated by inputting the data into a scientific calculator. By using pre-programmed keys the standard deviation can be found. Make sure you know how to do this on your calculator.

The more complete example in Representing Data in Diagrams (pages 14–17) should help explain this further.

Generally, when comparing two sets of data, a lower standard deviation implies more consistency within the set.

SUMMARY

- Quantitative data can be presented numerically by:
  - measures of the centre, i.e.
    - mean – all values are added and divided by the sample size
    - mode – the most frequently occurring item or class interval
    - median – the middle data point when all values are arranged in numerical order
  - measures of spread, i.e.
    - range – highest minus lowest numbers
    - IQR – upper quartile minus lower quartile or middle 50%.
- Standard deviation (σ) is the 'mean distance' from the mean.
- When comparing two data sets, a lower standard deviation implies greater consistency within that set.

QUICK TEST

Use the following data set for Questions 1–3:
12, 12, 14, 15, 15, 15 and 17

1. Find **a)** the mean, **b)** the mode and **c)** the median of the data set.

2. Find **a)** the range, **b)** the IQR and **c)** the standard deviation of the data set.

3. What percentage of the data does the IQR involve and where is this data located?

4. A survey conducted of the number of bedrooms in 100 houses produced the following results.

Number of Bedrooms	1	2	3	4	5	6
Frequency	17	33	26	14	6	4

Calculate the standard deviation.

PRACTICE QUESTIONS

1. The global percentage of people with Internet access is averaged at around 40% per country. In one country, 85% of people have access, which represents 2.5 standard deviations above the mean.

   What is the global standard deviation? **[2 marks]**

2. The mean number of children per household in the UK is 1.8 and the standard deviation is 0.78.

   Is it possible to have a number of children more than three standard deviations from the mean? Explain your answer. **[4 marks]**

3. Two machines make small nuts for screws.
   A sample of nuts is taken from each machine and the width of each nut is recorded in mm.

A	2.27	2.31	2.18	2.2	2.26	2.24	–	–	–
B	2.78	2.62	2.61	2.51	2.59	2.67	2.62	2.68	2.70

   a) Find the mean and standard deviation for each machine. **[4 marks]**

   b) Which machine is most consistent?
   Give a reason for your answer. **[2 marks]**

4. The table shows the mean BMI (body mass index) for 10 countries. It was obtained from the Gapminder website (https://www.gapminder.org).

Country	BMI
Afghanistan	20.62
Angola	22.25
Australia	27.56
Austria	26.47
Azerbaijan	25.65
Bahamas	27.25
Bangladesh	20.40
Belgium	26.76
Bolivia	24.43
Botswana	22.13

   a) What type of data is this? **[2 marks]**

   b) Calculate the mean and standard deviation for the data. **[2 marks]**

   c) An Australian journalist claims that the global average BMI is now around 24 and that Australians are the heaviest in the world.

   Is that a correct interpretation of the data given? Give a reason for your answer. **[2 marks]**

Representing Data in Diagrams

LEARNING OBJECTIVES

You need to be able to:

● construct appropriate diagrams for grouped discrete data and continuous data

● interpret diagrams for grouped discrete data and continuous data and reach conclusions based on them.

You should know about pictograms, bar charts (including composite bar charts), pie charts and scatter graphs from GCSE.

You also need to about the following types of diagram in more detail:

Diagram	Description	Advantages	Disadvantages
Stem-and-Leaf Diagram	Uses columns to represent the stem (often tens) and rows for the leaves (often units). A key is given to help read the inputs. **Example** 19, 20, 23, 21, 27, 31, 33 becomes (in ascending order): <table><tr><td>1</td><td>9</td></tr><tr><td>2</td><td>0 1 3 7</td></tr><tr><td>3</td><td>1 3</td></tr></table> Key: 1|9 means 19	Good for small data sets – shows the shape of the distribution. Useful for finding the median.	Time-consuming and less clear for large data sets.
Back-to-Back Stem-and-Leaf Diagram	Data sets have the same stem and the leaves run back-to-back.	Can be used for comparing two data sets.	
Box and Whisker Plot	A rectangular box is used to represent the lower and upper quartiles and median within a data set, whilst straight lines (whiskers) extend to the lowest and highest values.	Shows range, IQR, median and extent of skew. Useful for comparing the above aspects of two or more sets of data.	Other work required before the plot can be constructed, i.e. finding the values for Q_1, Q_2 and Q_3.

Cumulative Frequency Graph	Produced by plotting the upper class boundary against the cumulative frequency (the running total). Produces an S-shaped curve (ogive). See example on next page.	Useful if source data is unsure or lost. Can give estimates of median and quartiles.	Only estimates can be achieved, as source data is not available.
Histogram	Used for grouped continuous data. The area of each bar represents (proportionately) the frequency of the class interval. The vertical axis is **frequency density** (fd): $\text{fd} = \dfrac{\text{frequency}}{\text{class width}}$	Gives a proportional representation of each class interval within the distribution. Median and quartiles can be estimated.	Only estimates can be achieved.

Example

A random sample of 40 runners was selected from the entrants in a marathon.
Their heights were recorded in metres.

Height, x (m)	Frequency	Cumulative Frequency
$1.75 \leq x < 1.80$	1	1
$1.80 \leq x < 1.85$	1	2
$1.85 \leq x < 1.90$	4	
$1.90 \leq x < 1.95$	13	
$1.95 \leq x < 2.00$	14	
$2.00 \leq x < 2.05$	3	
$2.05 \leq x < 2.10$	3	
$2.10 \leq x < 2.15$	1	

a) Complete the cumulative frequency column of the table.

Cumulative frequency is a running total, e.g. the cumulative frequency for the class interval $1.85 \leq x < 1.90$ is $1 + 1 + 4 = 6$ (the total frequency for that class, plus all those that precede it).

So, from top to bottom the missing values are: 6, 19, 33, 36, 39 and 40

b) Construct a cumulative frequency curve for the data.

To plot the curve, you use the upper class boundary and the cumulative frequency.

So the points should be plotted at (1.80, 1), (1.85, 2), (1.90, 6), (1.95, 19), (2.00, 33), (2.05, 36), (2.10, 39) and (2.15, 40) and joined by a smooth S-shaped curve.

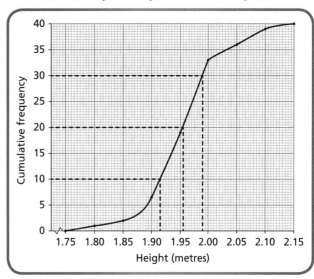

c) Use your cumulative frequency curve to estimate:

i) the median (Q_2)

There are 40 values, so the median is the 20th value. Draw a line across from 20 on the y-axis to the curve and then down to the x-axis.
$Q_2 = 1.955$

ii) the upper quartile (Q_3)

The upper quartile is the 30th value, so:
$Q_3 = 1.99$

iii) the lower quartile (Q_1)

The upper lower is the 10th value, so:
$Q_1 = 1.915$

d) Compare your values of ($Q_3 - Q_2$) and ($Q_2 - Q_1$) and explain what this indicates about the shape of the distribution.

$Q_3 - Q_2 = 0.035$ and $Q_2 - Q_1 = 0.04$, so the distribution is not symmetrical

SUMMARY

● **There are many different diagrams that can be used to present data:**

○ **stem-and-leaf diagram** – uses columns for the stem and rows for the leaves
○ **back-to-back stem-and-leaf diagram** – used to compare two data sets back-to-back
○ **box and whisker plot** – shows lower quartile, median, upper quartile and range
○ **cumulative frequency graph** – an S-shaped curve that shows a running total of scores
○ **histogram** – the area of each bar represents the frequency.

QUICK TEST

1. Explain the difference between back-to-back and normal stem-and-leaf diagrams.

2. What are the main features of a box and whisker plot?

3. What is cumulative frequency?

4. What do the bars in a histogram represent?

PRACTICE QUESTIONS

1. The heights of the buildings in a street are given below, in metres:
482, 501, 572, 658, 450, 505, 452, 486, 504, 452, 508, 454

    a) Draw a stem-and-leaf diagram for this data.   **[2 marks]**

    b) What is the height of the second tallest building?   **[1 mark]**

    c) What is the range of the given data?   **[1 mark]**

    d) How many buildings have the same height?   **[1 mark]**

    e) What is the difference in height between the third tallest and the fifth tallest building?   **[1 mark]**

    f) What is the mean height of buildings on the street?   **[2 marks]**

2. Pupils applying for a place at a grammar school were asked to complete a test.
The cumulative frequency graph gives the test results of the 120 applicants.

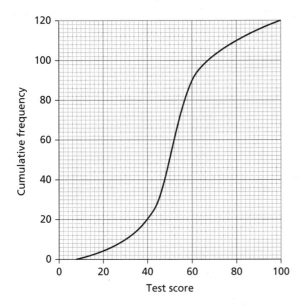

    a) Use the graph to find:

        i) the median score   **[2 marks]**

        ii) the interquartile range   **[2 marks]**

    b) The school will only accept the top 40% of applicants.

    What is the mark achieved by the top 40%?   **[2 marks]**

Numerical Calculations

LEARNING OBJECTIVES

You need to be able to:

- calculate using formulae, spreadsheets and financial expressions
- use conventional notation for order of operations
- apply and interpret limits of accuracy
- find approximate solutions to problems in financial contexts.

A basic understanding of personal finance is something that can benefit everyone.

As with all topics in Level 3 Maths, you must be able to apply your knowledge and skills in real-world contexts, so there are some commonly used concepts and jargon that you need to understand.

BIDMAS (or BODMAS)

In all calculations, operations must be carried out in **BIDMAS** order:

1. **B**rackets
2. **I**ndices (e.g. powers, squares, roots, etc.) or **O**thers (e.g. trig functions)
3. **D**ivision and/or **M**ultiplications
4. **A**dditions and/or **S**ubtractions.

Example

Can you tell what operations are needed in the following calculations so they are correct?

$3 + 4 \times 6 = 42$ should be $(3 + 4)\,6 = 42$

$5 + 6 = 31$ should be $5^2 + 6 = 31$

$95 \ 5 + 8 \ 3 = 30$ should be $(95 \div 5) + 8 + 3 = 30$

Spreadsheets and Financial Expressions

All spreadsheets should be programmed with BIDMAS (or BODMAS) in mind.

Formulae in spreadsheets reference the cell(s) containing the items to be used, e.g. A1, B2, etc.

You should already understand and be able to apply some formulae, e.g.

- =D1+E3+F9 (adds the values in the cells)
- =G13*B17 (multiplies the values in the cells)
- =(D15 + C3)/E2*100 (where / means divide)
- =Sum(D1:D9) (totals all the values in the cell range)

Example

Look at the spreadsheet.

A	B	C	D
1	Sale		250000.00
2	Purchase		169000.00
3			
4	Capital Gain		81000.00
5			
6	Allowable Costs		
7	Stamp Duty	1690.00	
8	VAT	295.75	
9	Solicitors etc.	6000.00	
10	Improvement	6000.00	
11			13985.75
12			
13	Taxable Gain		67014.25
14	Less Allowable Gain		10100.00
15	Net Taxable Gain		56914.25
16			
17	Tax at 18%		10244.57
18	First half payment		5122.28

What formula has been used in each of these cells?

a) D4 = D1−D2   c) D17 = D15*0.18

b) D11 = Sum(C7:C10)   d) $D18 = \frac{(D17)}{2}$

Accuracy and its Limits

Rounding

Because physical amounts of money (in pounds) can only be given to two decimal places, most financial calculations or conclusions are rounded, e.g. an amount of £567.987654 is normally rounded to £567.99.

Interval Errors

Where a figure of £315 is given to the nearest pound:

- the **lower bound** is £314.50
- the **upper bound** is £315.50
- there is an **interval error** of £0.50

Truncating

Values in tax calculations are often **truncated**, i.e. the numbers are cut off at a certain point without rounding.

E.g. if your income is £356.98, it is truncated to £356.

Approximation

Sometimes you need to calculate an approximate cost.

Example

A weekly bus ticket costs £17.

A college year is 195 days with two weeks off over the Christmas period.

Roughly how much will Sam need to spend on bus transport to and from college each year?

$\frac{195}{7}$ is approximately 28 weeks; 28 − 2 = 26 weeks

Approximate cost: 25 weeks × £20 ≈ £500.

SUMMARY

- Follow BIDMAS in all calculations.

- You must be able to read spreadsheets and input formulae.

- When rounding to a given level of accuracy (e.g. 2 decimal places or the nearest unit, 10 or 100), look at the appropriate digit and round up if it's 5 or above, and down if it's below 5.

- Rounding creates interval errors and the lower/upper bounds must be considered.

- A truncated number is cut off at a certain point without rounding.

- Approximation can take many forms, but generally all values are rounded to one or two significant figures for ease of calculations.

PRACTICE QUESTIONS

1. Revenue from a new product is estimated to be around £30 000 based on sales of 333 units at £90.45 each.

   Calculate the real value of sales and the percentage error on the estimate. **[3 marks]**

2. Look at the spreadsheet:

	A	B	C	D	E
1	Year	Start Amount	Interest Rate	Interest Earned	Total at Year End
2	1	1000	5%	50	1050
3	2	1050	5%	52.5	1102.5
4	3	1102.5	5%	55.125	1157.625
5					

   a) Write the formula used in cell E2. **[1 mark]**

   b) What formula could be input in cell D5 to calculate the total interest earned in 3 years? **[1 mark]**

   c) What calculation could be performed on the value in B2 to obtain the value in D4? **[1 mark]**

Percentages

Percentages – GCSE Revision

Percentages as Fractions or Decimals

Percentage	34%	0.25%	55.2%	359%
Fraction	$\frac{34}{100} = \frac{17}{50}$	$\frac{25}{10000} = \frac{1}{400}$	$\frac{552}{1000} = \frac{69}{125}$	$\frac{359}{100} = 3\frac{59}{100}$
Decimal	0.34	0.0025	0.552	3.59

A Percentage of a Quantity

What is 35% of £145?

$\frac{35}{100} \times 145 = £50.75$ or $0.35 \times 145 = £50.75$

One Quantity as a Percentage of Another

£200 out of £800 is paid in tax. What percentage is this?

$\frac{200}{800} \times 100 = 25\%$

Comparing Two Quantities

A salary of £22 000 is increased by £660 and a salary of £48 000 is increased by £1000.

Which is the highest percentage increase?

Salary of £22 000 increase $= \frac{660}{22000} \times 100 = 3\%$

Salary of £48 000 increase $= \frac{1000}{48000} \times 100 = 2.08\%$

The salary of £22 000 is increased by the highest percentage.

Percentage Increases (Appreciation)
Increasing an Amount

What is £150 increased by 15%?

100% + 15% = 115%

150 × 1.15 = £172.50

Finding the Original Value

The value of an apartment increases by 12% to £125 000.

What was the original price to the nearest pound?

New price = £125 000 = 112%

Original price (100%) $= \frac{125\,000}{112} \times 100 = £111\,607$

Percentage Decreases (Depreciation)
Decreasing an Amount

What is £210 decreased by 15%?

100% − 15% = 85%

210 × 0.85 = £178.50

Finding the Original Value

A pair of jeans is priced at £59.50 after a 30% reduction.

What was the original price?

100% − 30% = 70%

New price (70%) = £59.50

Original price (100%) $= \frac{59.50}{70} \times 100 = £85$

SUMMARY

Percentages can:

- ○ be expressed as decimals and fractions
- ○ be used to compare two transactions
- ○ help with calculating increases and decreases.

QUICK TEST

1. Express 45% as a fraction in its simplest form and a decimal.

2. Work out 64% and 73.8% of £518.

3. Express 15 out of 46 as a percentage. Give your answer to three decimal places.

4. In Shop A, the price of a pair of jeans is reduced from £99 by £12.

   In Shop B, the same pair of jeans is reduced from £75 by £8.

   Which is the greatest percentage decrease?

5. Express the following multiples as percentages:

   a) 1.45

   b) 2.67

6. What is £450 worth after an increase of 12% followed by a decrease of 10.7%?

7. A car's value is £5600 after a depreciation of 20%. What was its original value?

PRACTICE QUESTIONS

1. The recipes for two lemonade drinks are shown in the table below.

	Lemon Juice (ml)	Fizzy Water (ml)	Sugar Syrup (ml)
Drink A	215	1750	35
Drink B	80	500	20

   a) What percentage of Drink A is lemon juice?
   [1 mark]

   b) Showing suitable calculations, determine which of the two drinks contains the greatest percentage of lemon juice? **[2 marks]**

   c) If Drink A and Drink B are combined, what is the percentage of lemon juice in the new mixture? **[2 marks]**

   d) 100 ml of lemon juice costs £0.20, 1 litre of fizzy water costs £0.40 and 35 ml of sugar syrup cost 17p.

   What is the cost of making 100 litres of Drink A? **[3 marks]**

   e) What should the selling prices be for one litre of Drink A to make an overall profit of 30%? **[2 marks]**

2. The table below shows the sale price and the deduction that it represents for several items.

Item	Sale Price	Deduction
Antenna	£12.99	13%
Mobile Phone	£49.99	53%
Gaming Laptop	£859.99	$42\frac{2}{3}$ %

   What was the price of each item before the sale?
   [4 marks]

Interest Rates

LEARNING OBJECTIVES

You need to be able to:

● perform calculations involving simple and compound interest rates

● understand the impact of interest rates on savings and investments, student loans and mortgages

● set up, solve and interpret the solutions to financial problems.

Simple Interest and Compound Interest

Simple interest is calculated based on the original investment amount, so the same amount of interest is earned each year (no interest is earned on the interest).

Compound interest is where interest is also earned on the interest paid in previous years.

Example

£1000 is invested in an account at 5% interest per year.

a) Calculate how much the investment is worth after 3 years if simple interest is paid.

Interest earned each year = £1000 × 0.05 = £50

3 × £50 = £150

Value after 3 years = £1000 + £150 = £1150

b) Calculate how much the investment is worth after 3 years if compound interest is paid.

Table Method

Year	Start Amount	Interest Rate	Interest Earned	Year End Total
1	£1000.00	5%	£50.00	£1050.00
2	£1050.00	5%	£52.50	£1102.50
3	£1102.50	5%	£55.13	£1157.63

Calculation Method

Value after 3 years = £1000 × $(1.05)^3$

= £1157.63

Simple Interest	$A = p + prt$
Compound Interest	$A = p \times (1 + r)^t$

Where:

● A is the future amount or value
● p is the principal (or original) amount
● r is the interest rate expressed as a decimal (e.g. 5% = 0.05)
● t is time (often in years or months)

Example

After 4 years, the value of a £2000 investment is worth £2800.

What was the interest rate?

A = £2800, P = £2000, $t = 4$ and r needs to be found.

Simple Interest

$2800 = 2000 + 2000r4$

$2800 - 2000 = 8000r$

$\dfrac{800}{8000} = r$

$r = 0.1 = 10\%$

Compound Interest

$2800 = 2000 \times (1 + r)^4$

$\dfrac{2800}{2000} = (1 + r)^4$

$\sqrt[4]{\dfrac{2800}{2000}} = (1 + r)$

$1.08776 = 1 + r$

$r = 0.08776 = 8.776\%$

AER (Annual Equivalent Rate)

AER is an overall annual rate used to make comparisons between savings accounts only. It uses the compound interest formula and often refers to monthly or weekly (or even daily or hourly) compounding.

Example

Calculate the AER for an investment rate of 5% per annum compounded weekly.

As the nominal (simple) annual rate is 5% per year, this needs to be divided by 52 to obtain the weekly rate. Here the sum invested can be assumed to be £1.

$A = P \times (1 + r)^t$

$A = 1 \times (1 + \frac{0.05}{52})^{52} = 1.051245842$ (remember, this is the invested amount plus interest)

So, the AER = 5.125% (to 3 dp), which is greater than 5%.

Generally the AER (r) is given by $r = (1 + \frac{i}{n})^n - 1$, where i is the nominal interest (in decimal form) and n is the number of compounding periods per year. This formula is provided on the formulae sheet in the exam.

APR (Annual Percentage Rate)

APR is similar to the AER but is generally used for borrowing, e.g. loans, mortgages and credit cards. Normally any extra costs (such as fees or other charges) are included but, for the purpose of this course, they are ignored.

Borrowing on credit cards is usually subject to APR.

$$C = \sum_{k=1}^{m} \left(\frac{A_k}{(1+i)^{tk}} \right)$$

Where:

- C is the amount of the loan
- m is the number of repayments
- i is the APR expressed as a decimal
- A_K is the amount of the kth repayment
- t_K is the interval in years between the start of the loan and kth repayment.

This formula is provided on the Formulae Sheet in the exam.

Example

A sum of £1000 is borrowed at an APR of 17% and is paid back in five equal monthly installments.

How much is the monthly payment?

$C = 1000$, $m = 5$, $i = 0.17$, t_k is a fraction with a denominator of 12 (as there are 12 months in a year) and A needs to be found.

As the payments are equal:

$$1000 = \frac{A}{(1.17)^{\frac{1}{12}}} + \frac{A}{(1.17)^{\frac{2}{12}}} + \frac{A}{(1.17)^{\frac{3}{12}}} + \frac{A}{(1.17)^{\frac{4}{12}}} + \frac{A}{(1.17)^{\frac{5}{12}}}$$

$$1000 = A \left(\frac{1}{(1.17)^{\frac{1}{12}}} + \frac{1}{(1.17)^{\frac{2}{12}}} + \frac{1}{(1.17)^{\frac{3}{12}}} + \frac{1}{(1.17)^{\frac{4}{12}}} + \frac{1}{(1.17)^{\frac{5}{12}}} \right)$$

$1000 = A \times (0.987 + 0.9742 + 0.9612 + 0.949 + 0.937)$

$A = \frac{1000}{4.80837} = 207.9707 = £207.97$

(Total repayment = £1039.85)

Students Loans

Student loans are used to help pay for higher or further education and generally contain elements such as:

- tuition fees (the costs of the course)
- maintenance loans (for living costs such as accommodation, books, bills, etc.)
- maintenance grants (cover the same aspects but do not need to be paid back).

Interest rates and tuition fees can vary from year to year. The values you should use in calculations will be provided on the exam paper or within the Preliminary Material.

Like all loans, student loans need repaying. Repayments start when you begin earning £21 000 or more.

The government provides the following guidelines for working out monthly payments on earnings above £21 000.

Calculation	Example: £31 500 Salary
1. Subtract £21 000 from annual salary	£31 500 – £21 000 = £10 500
2. Calculate 9% of the remainder	£10 500 × 0.09 = £945
3. Divide by 12	$\dfrac{£945}{12} = £78.75$
4. Truncate to pounds only	£78 per month

Like all loans, student loans have to be repaid, but repayments only start once you earn £21 000 or more.

The outstanding amount will include yearly interest on the initial loan. This is dependent on a number of variables. Below is a general overview.

Period	Interest Rate
The duration of your studies up until the April after you finish or leave your course	**Retail Price Index (RPI)** + 3%
From the April after you finish or leave your course onwards	Interest will be based on your income: £21 000 or less = RPI £21 000–£41 000 = RPI + up to 3% (depending on income) £41 000+ = RPI + 3%

Example

A graduate has an outstanding student loan of £30 000.

They begin a job with a starting salary of £29 000, which increases by £2000 each year.

Assuming the RPI is 2%, what is the maximum monthly repayment that the graduate will have to make for years 1, 2 and 3 and what is the outstanding balance for each of these years?

Year	Outstanding Loan Balance Year Begin	5% Max Interest (2% RPI + Max of 3%)	Income	Income Above £21 000	Annual Payment (9% of Income Above £21 000)	Outstanding Balance Year End
1	£30 000.00	£1500.00	£29 000.00	£8000.00	£720.00	£30 780.00
2	£30 780.00	£1539.00	£31 000.00	£10 000.00	£900.00	£31 419.00
3	£31 419.00	£1570.95	£33 000.00	£12 000.00	£1080.00	£31 909.95

The monthly payment for Year 1 is $\frac{£720}{12} = £60$, Year 2 is $\frac{£900}{12} = £75$ and Year 3 is $\frac{£1080}{12} = £90$. The outstanding balance for each is shown in the 'Year End' column.

If the spreadsheet were extended, it should show that the outstanding loan only drops below £30 000 in Year 11.

Mortgages

As with the example above, when you take out a mortgage or loan to buy a house or property, it usually takes a long time before the initial capital loan starts to reduce.

Affordability (or eligibility) is usually determined by:

Criteria	Definition	Example
Income Multiple	The multiple of income that a lender will allow for a given loan or mortgage.	If a couple has a combined yearly income of £42 000 and the maximum multiple allowed is 4.5, then the maximum mortgage is £42 000 × 4.5 = £189 000
Loan to Value (LTV)	The percentage of the sale value of the property for which a mortgage is required or allowed. This can vary from lender to lender.	If a mortgage of £100 000 is required for a £150 000 property, then the LTV $= \frac{100}{150} \times 100 = 67\%$ Here, there is a 33% deposit or equity to cover the balance.
Credit Rating	A measure of how trusted an applicant is to pay back a loan. Usually obtained from credit agencies or companies based on past records.	Varies according to the lender's criteria. Can be scored in various ways. Unlikely to be tested.
Outgoings or Expenses	The monthly outgoings taken out of the monthly income. The difference between income and outgoings is used as a basis of affordability.	If monthly take-home pay is £2000 and total outgoings (food, travel, clothes, entertainment, utilities, etc.) are £1200, then the maximum net income available for a mortgage = £2000 – £1200 = £800.

Repayments are usually based on equal monthly amounts, but interest is also added to the amount outstanding.

Example

The table shows calculations for a £175 000 mortgage for 35 years with a fixed rate of 1.79% for 3 years, reverting to 3.74% for the remaining years.

Year	Balance (A_{n+1})	Interest Rate	Annual Interest	Monthly Payment	Annual Payment	End of Year Balance
1	£175 000.00	1.94%	£3395.00	£574.34	£6892.08	£171 502.92
2	£171 502.92	1.94%	£3327.16	£574.34	£6892.08	£167 938.00
3	£167 938.00	1.94%	£3258.00	£574.34	£6892.08	£164 303.91
4	£164 303.91	3.74%	£6144.97	£733.96	£8807.52	£161 641.36

If A0 is the initial balance for Year 1 with A1 for Year 2, A2 for Year 3, etc. then A_n is the current year balance and A_{n+1} (the following year balance) is calculated as:

$A_{n+1} = A_n \times (1 + \text{interest rate}) - \text{annual payment}$

This is called a **recurrence relation**, as it is repeated or reiterated every year or period.

The monthly repayment is calculated from a formula that is beyond the requirements of this course. It takes into account lots of variables, including the principal, loan period, interest, taxes and insurance.

QUICK TEST

1. What is the difference between simple and compound interest?

2. What do AER and APR stand for and when are they used?

3. If £3000 is invested at 3% interest, how much is the investment worth after five years if the interest is compounded a) yearly and b) monthly?

4. What do student loans pay for?

5. What is a mortgage and what are the four criteria of affordability?

6. What is the LTV on a mortgage?

7. What is a recurrence relation?

PRACTICE QUESTIONS

1. Winnie invests £3000 in a savings account at a fixed rate of 3% compound interest per annum.

   How long will it take for her money to exceed £4000?   **[3 marks]**

2. Angika starts work with a salary of £19 000 and a student loan of £25 000.

   She must pay 9% of earnings above £21 000.

   Simple interest at 3% is added to the outstanding loan at the start of each year.

   If her salary increases by 5% each year, in what year will Angika start to repay her loan and what will the monthly payment be in that year?   **[3 marks]**

Other Financial Aspects

Taxation

There are two basic ways to be taxed:

● on income earned (e.g. a salary or wage or even an investment or savings account)
● **value added tax (VAT)**.

Income Tax

Income tax is a direct percentage charge on a salary or wage (usually monthly).

2016		
Current Band	**Taxable Income**	**Tax Rate**
Personal Allowance	Up to £11 000	0%
Basic Rate	£11 001 to £43 000	20%
Higher Rate	£43 001 to £150 000	40%
Additional Rate	Over £150 000	45%

Example
For a salary of £45 000 per year, what is **a)** the income tax payable on and **b)** the percentage tax on gross income?

Gross Income	£45 000
Personal Allowance	£11 000
Taxable Income (Gross – Personal Allowance)	£34 000
Tax @ 20% on first £32 000	£6400
Tax @ 40% on remaining £2000	£800
Total Income Tax Per Year	£7200
Monthly Tax	£600

This represents $\frac{7.2}{45} \times 100 = 16\%$ of the gross income.

National Insurance (NI)

National Insurance is a contribution made by everyone (age 16 years or over) who earns over a threshold amount. It qualifies them for certain benefits, including the State Pension and Jobseekers Allowance.

The rates for 2016–17 are shown in the table below:

Monthly Income	Class 1 NI
First £672 (£8064/year)	0%
Next £672 to £3583	12%
Over £3583	2%

Example
Calculate the monthly NI contribution for a salary of £45 000.

Monthly income on which NI is to be paid = $\frac{£45\,000 - £8064}{12} = £3078$

Monthly NI contribution = $0.12 \times £3078 = £369.36$.

For a salary of £45 000, total monthly deductions are £600 + £369.36 = £969.36 (£11 632.32 per year), which represents about 26% of gross income. Other deductions, including pension contributions, would increase this percentage.

Value Added Tax (VAT)

Value added tax (VAT) is a tax applied to most goods and services that are purchased by consumers. For most goods, it is charged at 20% and is added onto the wholesale price.

Rate	VAT (%)	Goods and Services
Standard	20%	Most goods and services
Reduced	5%	Example: children's car seats and home energy
Zero	0%	Example: books, most food and children's clothes

Example

Work out the VAT payable on:

a) a solicitor's net cost of £250 per hour

The solicitor's work is considered a service, so it is charged at 20% VAT.

VAT = £250 × 20% = £50, so the gross cost is £300 per hour.

b) a quarterly electricity bill of total £452

The £452 total includes the VAT (at 5%), so represents 105% of the net charge.

VAT = $\frac{452}{105}$ × 5 = £21.52, so the net charge before VAT is £430.48.

Inflation

Inflation is the rate of increase in prices for goods and services.

There are various measures of inflation. The **Retail Price Index (RPI)** and **Consumer Price Index (CPI)** are the ones most commonly used.

To track inflation, the Office of National Statistics (ONS) collects data each month on more than 100 000 goods and services, and considers the weighting of different items in the overall calculation.

The Bank of England has a target to try and keep inflation at around 2%.

Example

The weekly State Pension of £119.30 is increased in line with the CPI of 1.5%.

What is the value after the increase?

New State Pension = £119.30 × 1.015 = £121.09 per week

Exchange Rates

An **exchange rate** is the cost of one currency compared to another, i.e. how much one unit (say £1) will buy of another currency at a particular time.

Exchange rates can vary minute-by-minute but are often shown on a day-to-day basis. They also vary according to:

- the **buy rate**, i.e. how much foreign currency is needed to buy one unit of local currency
- the **sell rate**, i.e. how much foreign currency is sold for every one unit of local currency.

Example

A bank is offering the following exchange rates for £1:

Currency	Buy	Sell
US$	1.30	1.23
Euro	1.20	1.12

a) How many US$ can be bought with £500?

£500 × 1.23 = $615

b) If the US$ are then changed back, how many GB£ do they buy?

$\frac{\$615}{1.30}$ = £442.80.

This results in a loss of £500 − £473.92 = £26.92. This is a very expensive exchange, which some consumers are unaware of.

Budgeting

The Chancellor of the Exchequer announces the Budget every year, which details the amount the Government intends to spend and how it will get its revenue from taxes and savings.

Likewise, all households should be aware of the balance between monthly income and spending. The process of planning so that spending does not exceed income is called budgeting.

Balancing the budget is where expenses are equal to income. When income exceeds expenses, it represents profit for businesses and savings for households.

Example

A student receives a maintenance loan of £8200 for one year and has the following expenses:

Expense	Weekly
Rent	£100
Food	£20
Books	£5
Electricity	£5
Going out/Entertainment	£30

Is this sustainable? Explain your answer.

Total spending per year = £160 × 52 = £8320

Total income from loan = £8200

Shortfall = £120

This may be sustainable if the shortfall can be pushed into the next year, but it will need to be covered eventually.

Alternatively, the shortfall could be reduced by taking a part-time job to increase income or by reducing entertainment expenses.

Graphical Representation

The most commonly used graphs for financial data are bar charts, pie charts and line graphs.

Example

Analyse the following graph and comment on the sustainability of household debt.

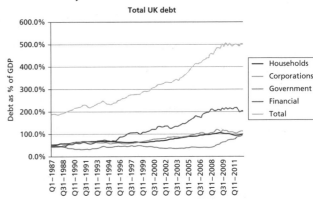

- All debt has risen since 1987, generally in a linear fashion.
- Household debt shows the sharpest rise, from 200% to 500%, representing around a 10% increase each year (if linear).
- Government debt was steady at around 40% but rose sharply from 2008 (following the financial crisis).
- As all sectors have debt at over 100% of the GDP (gross domestic product), it is questionable whether this is sustainable. This is particularly true for household debt.

QUICK TEST

1. What is income tax and how much would be paid on a salary of £11 200?
2. What is the maximum weekly wage before National Insurance is payable?
3. Calculate the VAT charged on a car with a wholesale price of £12 000.
4. How many goods do the ONS collect data on to help measure inflation?
5. Explain the difference between the buy rate and sell rate for a currency.
6. How many US$ will £100 buy at a sell rate of £1 = $1.45?
7. Explain what 'balancing the budget' means.
8. What types of graph are used in financial maths?

PRACTICE QUESTIONS

1. Use the table below to answer the following questions.

Current Band	Taxable Income	Tax Rate
Personal allowance	Up to £11 000	0%
Basic rate	£11 001 to £43 000	20%
Higher rate	£43 001 to £150 000	40%
Additional rate	Over £150 000	45%

    a) Calculate the tax paid on a salary of £48 000.   **[3 marks]**

    b) What percentage of the above salary is not subject to income tax?   **[1 mark]**

    c) Calculate the flat rate of tax paid (actual percentage of tax paid on total income) on a salary of £48 000.   **[1 mark]**

2. Work out the VAT for a service included on a bill for £4500.   **[2 marks]**

3. A bank offers a buy rate of £1 = $1.22 and a sell rate of £1 = $1.15

    a) Calculate how many US$ can be bought with £1000.   **[2 marks]**

    b) If the actual rate is the midpoint between the buy and sell rate (the mid-rate), what is the percentage profit on the sell rate for the bank?   **[3 marks]**

4. The table below shows the typical cost of a burger in three countries.

Canada (Can$)	5.93
USA (US$)	5.04
UK (GB£)	2.97

If the exchange rate is 1 US$ = £0.753 = 1.29 Can$, in which country is the burger most expensive?   **[3 marks]**

5. If the Consumer Price Index (CPI) has had an average yearly inflation rate of 2% over the last 10 years, what would a basket of goods costing £540 today have cost 10 years ago?   **[2 marks]**

6. Write down three things that can be deduced from the chart showing government revenue and expenditure as a percentage of GDP (Gross Domestic Product).   **[3 marks]**

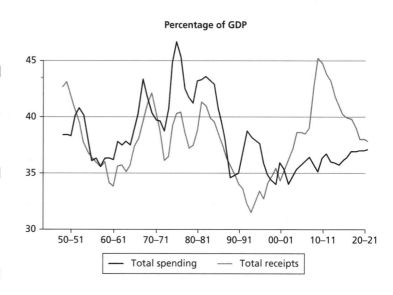

Percentage of GDP

— Total spending   — Total receipts

Using Models

LEARNING OBJECTIVES

You need to be able to:

- represent a situation mathematically, making assumptions and simplifications
- select and use appropriate techniques.

To make a calculation or estimate a quantity, it is generally necessary to represent the problem as a **model**. This will involve some **simplifications** and **assumptions**.

For example, in most calculations, the Earth can be considered to be a sphere, even though it is slightly wider at the equator. It is modelled as a perfectly round object.

Estimation can involve a number of techniques.

This section splits the techniques into parts, to reinforce the different tools available for problem-solving. For example, the **Fermi estimate** process (pages 40–41) is just another way of approaching **estimates**. It is not a distinct technique

The typical process for modelling is as follows:

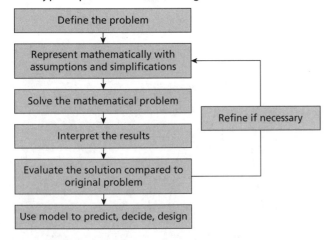

Questions on estimation will include marks for stating any simplifications and assumptions that are made, as well as marks for the calculations and correct answer(s).

Some questions will give very little in the way of information, so it is helpful to have some starting points, such as:

Mass:

Human adult:	75 kg
Family car:	1500 kg
Kilogram:	2.2 pounds (double and add 10%)

Length:

Earth's radius:	6370 km
Adult height:	1.7 m
Length of Great Britain:	1000 km (1400 km by road) from Land's End to John O'Groats
London to Birmingham:	100 miles or 160 km (conversion 1:1.6)
1 foot:	30 cm

Volume:

Can of drink:	330 ml (Europe)
1 m^3:	1000 litres
1 gallon:	4.5 litres

Density: $\dfrac{mass}{volume}$ (water = 1 kg/m^3)

Time:

Human lifespan:	75 years
Days in a year:	365
Weeks in a year:	52
Hours in a day:	24

Speed:

Human walk:	3 mph (fast 4 mph)
Human sprint:	30 mph (Usain Bolt – 27.8 mph)
1 mph:	0.45 m/s (to convert, halve and subtract 10%)

Other:

Population of the world: 7.5 billion
Population of London: 8.7 million
Population of UK: 65 million

Please note that throughout this section, the examples and answers given are *not* the only possible way of responding to the questions. There are a number of different and valid approaches to the solution.

Example

How long will it take an air-conditioning unit to replace the air in a typical room?

Assumptions and simplifications:

Shape of room:	cuboid
Size of room:	5 m × 7 m × 2.5 m
Rate of air flow through air-conditioning unit:	1 litre per second, assume also that this is constant (Imagine that the air coming into the room is water filling a bottle – a litre bottle could be filled in one second.)
Number of litres in a cubic metre:	1000 litres (This is not strictly an assumption, but some estimations of quantities will be in different units and you will need to convert between them.)

Assume that the air-conditioning changes all the air in the room, not just the same part of the air repeatedly.

Calculation:

Volume of room:	$5 \times 7 \times 2.5 = 87.5$ m^3
Work in same units:	87.5 m^3 × 1000 = 87 500 litres
Time to change air:	$\dfrac{\text{volume (litres)}}{\text{time taken to change 1 litre}} =$ $\dfrac{87\,500}{1} = 87\,500$ seconds
Give answer in reasonable units:	87 500 seconds $= \dfrac{87\,500}{60} =$ 1458.3 minutes = 24.3 hours = 1 day

Example

How many times does a person blink in a lifetime?

Assumptions and simplifications:

Frequency of blink:	15 times a minute
Human lifespan:	75 years
Time awake:	16 hours a day

Calculation:

Blinks per day:	$15 \times 60 \times 16 = 14\,400$
Days in lifetime:	$365 \times 75 = 27\,375$
Total number of blinks:	$14\,400 \times 27\,375 \approx 400$ million

Example

How far does a person swim in a year?

Assumptions and simplifications:

Frequency of swimming:	once a week (reasonably well-off city dweller)
Duration of each swim:	one hour
Swimming speed:	a little less than 1 m/s (Consider walking at the speed of swimming or the time it takes to swim 25 m.)

Calculation:

Time in pool per year:	50 weeks × 1 hour × 60 minutes × 60 seconds = 180 000 seconds
Distance travelled:	speed × time = 1 m/s × 180 000 seconds ≈ 150 km (if less than 1 m/s)

Example

How long would it take one person to move a mountain?

This one is more challenging. Work through it systematically.

Assumptions and simplifications:

Size of mountain:	a cone of height 1000 m and radius 1000 m
Human lifespan:	75 years
Hours worked:	16 hours a day (all waking hours to give the fastest possible time)
Method:	use a dumper truck to move rock to a site 2 km away
Size of each load:	1000 kg
Loading time:	5 kg/s
Density of rock:	2.5 kg/m³ (rock sinks, so maybe two and half times the density of water)

Calculation:

Time to fill truck:	$\frac{1000}{5} = 200$ s
Time to move truck and return:	4 km at 20 km/h, plus emptying = 15 minutes
Time to move 1000 kg:	20 mins, therefore 3 tonnes/hour
Volume of mountain:	$\frac{1}{3}\pi \times r^2 \times h = 1 \times 10^9$ m³
Mass of mountain:	$1 \times 10^9 \times 2.5$ kg/m³ $= 2.5 \times 10^9$ kg
Time taken:	$\frac{2.5 \times 10^9}{3000} = 667\,000$ hours
Time taken in days:	$\frac{667\,000}{24} = 28\,000$ days
Time taken in years:	$\frac{28\,000}{365} \approx 75$ years (A lifetime well spent, although it would probably take longer and you might want to consider the years that a person is unable to work because they are too young or old.)

QUICK TEST

How could the following examples be modelled?

Give the assumptions and simplifications only. The calculation and solution is not needed.

1. A family collects their food waste in a pile in the garden. How tall is the pile after one year?

2. How much time do people spend commuting to work in a lifetime?

3. How many childcare providers are there in Birmingham?

4. How long would it take someone to read all the books in their local library?

5. What is the surface area of the human body?

6. A report says that the average Briton spends 43 months in education in their lifetime. Is this true?

7. How much water is supplied to a block of flats per day?

8. How long does it take to complete one circuit of the M25?

9. What is the kinetic energy of the Earth moving around the sun?

   (Kinetic energy is the energy due to movement, $E = \frac{1}{2} \times \text{mass} \times \text{velocity}^2$)

PRACTICE QUESTIONS

1. How much water does a person drink in one year?   **[5 marks]**

2. Could the population of the world fit on the Isle of Wight?   **[8 marks]**

3. How much tax is collected by the government on the sale of petrol every year?
(Assume a car travels 40 miles to the gallon and petrol costs £1.10 per litre.)   **[9 marks]**

4. How many escalators would be needed to move all the people getting off a Eurostar
train down to passport control in less than one minute?   **[5 marks]**

DAY 3 ⏱ 60 Minutes

Interpreting and Evaluating Results

There are quick ways of doing estimations, such as **Fermi estimates** (see pages 40–41), and there are more involved, detailed methods that use more accurate representations and data.

Wherever possible, it is important to check the accuracy of the model and compare the results it produces with the data, e.g. if the model says the population doubles every ten years in a particular city, how well does this match the historical data?

Example
A fried chicken takeaway shop sells chicken at the following prices:

6 pieces:	£9.99
10 pieces:	£12.99
14 pieces:	£16.79

How much would 18 pieces cost?

Plotting the given data and drawing a line of best fit would give a value of about £20.

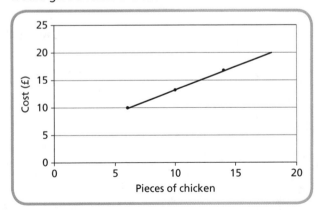

Alternatively, look at how the cost of an individual piece of chicken reduces with quantity:
6 pieces at £1.67 each
10 pieces at £1.30 each
14 pieces at £1.20 each

This might give 18 pieces at a cost of around £1.20 each and a total cost of around £21.60.

Different models will give different answers.

Perhaps the box of chicken also contains some chips and drinks, in which case having a linear increase in cost for additional chicken pieces (i.e. the first model) would be better.

If the price only includes the chicken, it is possible to imagine that buying in bulk would reduce the cost of the individual pieces of chicken, so the second model would be better.

Example
The following data shows the heart rates of various mammals.

Animal	Mass (kg)	Resting Heart Rate (bpm)	Lifespan (years)
Rabbit	1	205	9
Cat	2	150	15
Human	75	70	75
Elephant	5000	30	70

It would seem that the smaller the animal, the faster the heart beats and the shorter the lifespan.

There are, of course, a number of calculations that could be carried out. One example is given below.

It is possible to determine the total number of heartbeats in a lifetime for each of the animals:

Minutes in a year: $60 \times 24 \times 365$ $= 5.26 \times 10^5$

Rabbit: $205 \times 5.26 \times 10^5 \times 9$ $= 9.7 \times 10^8$
Cat: $150 \times 5.26 \times 10^5 \times 15 = 12 \times 10^8$
Human: $70 \times 5.26 \times 10^5 \times 75 = 28 \times 10^8$
Elephant: $30 \times 5.26 \times 10^5 \times 70 = 11 \times 10^8$

It would seem from this that mammals have about 1 billion heartbeats in their lifetime. Humans appear to be the exception. Maybe without science and medicine they would live only 30 years.

A dog's heart rate is 95 bpm. Is it possible to work out how long a dog might live from this model?

On the assumption that a dog has 1 billion heartbeats:

$$\text{Lifespan} = \frac{(1 \times 10^9)}{(95 \times 5.26 \times 10^5)} = 20 \text{ years}$$

Is this reasonable?

It is probably on the high side, but not too bad.

What is actually being assumed?

Quite a lot. For example, it assumes that the frequency of heart beats is regular. Whereas, when the animal is more active, the heart rate will actually go up.

Using the model, increased activity would shorten the animal's lifespan as it would be using up its 1 billion heart beats more quickly. In reality, the opposite is probably true, as biology suggests that taking exercise will prolong life.

It is further possible to obtain a relationship between the mass and the heart rate:

$H = 200 \, m^{-0.22}$, where H is the heart rate in bpm and m the mass in kg.

Using this formula, it is possible to estimate that the heart rate of a 6 kg monkey is about 135 bpm, which again seems reasonable.

What about extending this model to be used where only the length dimension is known?

It might be possible to assume that the animal is spherical and that the mass depends on the length cubed so that the model can be used.

What about extending the model to reptiles?

There could be a number of different factors in the biology of animals that determine the behavior of the heart. There may also be more significant variations in the shapes of different reptiles and this could affect the model. It would be necessary to analyse more data.

Example

Is the force of gravity the same at the bottom of a mineshaft as it is at the top of a mountain?

The deepest mineshaft is nearly 4 km (3.9) below the surface of the Earth and the tallest mountain is 8.8 km (8.85).

Given that the radius of the Earth is nearly 6400 km (6371), it would be reasonable to ignore the variation.

$$\frac{(8.85 + 3.9)}{6371} = 0.002 = 0.2\%$$

Whilst the distance varies by only 0.2% gravity depends on the distance squared, so this would actually result in a variation of 0.4% (a 0.2% increase is like multiplying by 1.002, so, $1.002^2 = 1.004$, i.e. a change of 0.4%), which is still small enough to ignore for most models.

If an object is modelled by a sphere, and for the purposes of a particular calculation it is only necessary to be accurate to within 10%, should it matter if the radius varies by 8%?

Yes, because if the radius increases by 8%, the volume will increase by 1.08^3, i.e. by 26%.

SUMMARY

- As before, it is important to make the following considerations when carrying out estimations:
  - ○ Are the simplifications and assumptions valid?
  - ○ By making certain choices, what is actually being assumed?
  - ○ What are the consequences of the simplifications and assumptions?
  - ○ What would change if the assumptions were changed?
  - ○ Can the assumptions be improved?
  - ○ Has all relevant data been considered?
  - ○ Are the results of the model sensible?
  - ○ Are the results only reasonable in a certain range?

QUICK TEST

1. A model has been developed to relate the floor area of a property to the sale price. Is it possible to use this in a different area of the town?

2. If a champagne bottle contains 1 litre, how much would a bottle twice as tall contain?

3. **a)** What factors could determine the maximum speed of a tennis serve?

   b) Which **two** factors are probably the most important?

4. Why would trying to determine the average number of attempts it takes someone to get a bull's-eye in darts not give a good answer?

5. Is it reasonable to assume the Earth is spherical?

6. A local politician says, 'An invasive species of beetle that kills a variety trees has been found in the local forest. Therefore, we must use all available resources to eliminate this pest as quickly as possible.' Why might this not be the best solution?

7. *If the price of my product is reduced, I will sell more and make more profit.* Is this always true?

8. Look at the image on the right. Is this always true?

THE BEST BREW

1 Add 200 ml of boiled water to your tea bag (in a mug)

2 Brew for 2 minutes

3 Remove the tea bag

4 Add 10 ml of milk

5 Wait six minutes for it to reach its optimum temperature of 60 °C

PRACTICE QUESTIONS

1. The following table shows the number of visits made by patients to a doctor's surgery in one year.

Number of Visits (v)	Frequency
$0 \leq v < 5$	5
$5 \leq v < 10$	47
$10 \leq v < 15$	11

   Estimate the mean number of visits.
   Show details of your assumptions and calculations.   **[4 marks]**

2. Samia has used the same taxi company twice.
   The first time it cost £10.50 for 4 miles.
   The second time it cost £22.50 for 10 miles.

   Estimate the cost for a 30-minute journey.
   Show details of your assumptions and calculations.   **[7 marks]**

3. How much space do all the bottles of cola sold in one day take up?   **[8 marks]**

4. A tidal barrier is to be built to generate electricity from the tides in a small river on the coast.
   There are two tides a day. The range between high and low tides is 4 m.
   The amount of energy in an object is given by the formula $E = mgh$, where m is mass,
   h is how high the object has been raised and g is gravity ($g = 9.81$ m/s^2).

   Estimate how much energy could be generated?   **[8 marks]**

Fermi Estimates

LEARNING OBJECTIVE

You need to be able to make fast, rough estimates of quantities that are either difficult or impossible to measure directly.

A **Fermi estimate** is a quick method of estimating a quantity, often used when there is little information available.

As with all questions, it is important to show your working, which in this case means the assumptions and simplifications.

The key idea is to have an answer that is the right order of magnitude (a multiple of ten), e.g. 20, not 2 or 200.

Techniques for solving Fermi estimate questions usually involve rounding quantities to make calculations easier.

This is sometimes done by considering the upper and lower bounds and breaking the problem down into parts that are known or can be estimated, or by comparing with known values.

Therefore, to create greater opportunity for comparison, it helps to have a decent general knowledge of typical values in the world around you (see pages 32–35 for some useful starters).

Example

How many trees are there in Parkhurst Forest on the Isle of Wight?

This is difficult because of lack of knowledge, but it can be broken down into elements that can be estimated:

How big is a forest? Perhaps 2 km × 2 km, which gives 4 km² or 4 000 000 m² (be careful when converting square and cubic units).

What is the distance between the trees? This could be estimated at 5 m.

If the trees are considered to be arranged in a grid, this would mean that each tree occupies a square of 25 m².

The number of trees is then $\frac{4\,000\,000}{25} = 160\,000$.

(The National Forestry Commission states that there are 150 000.)

Example

How much time per day does the average 15-year-old spend watching TV?

It can be difficult to know where to start, so sometimes it is easier to give maximum and minimum values, i.e. upper and lower bounds.

For example, it is definitely more than 2 minutes (lower bound) and less than 7 hours (upper bound), which can be rounded to 400 minutes.

As the difference between these values is over a factor of 100, taking a mean would be pointless.

A **geometric mean** can be used instead, to give an answer in the right order of magnitude (factor of ten).

The geometric mean is the square root of the product of the upper and lower bounds.

In standard form, 2 is 2×10^0 and 400 is 4×10^2. The average of the coefficients (2 and 4) is 3 and the average of the exponents (0 and 2) is 1. So, an approximate geometric mean of 2 and 400 is 3×10^1 or 30.

In the exam, you can use a calculator. This would give a precise geometric mean of $\sqrt{(2 \times 400)} = 28.28$ (30 minutes).

Finally, consider whether the solution is reasonable in the real world? Probably a little low, but it is in the right order of magnitude – the solution is unlikely to be 3 minutes or 300 minutes.

- Break the problem down into simpler parts that can be estimated.

- Use simple numbers and calculations to get a rough estimate.

- Consider using upper and lower bounds to find a geometric mean.

- Is the answer in the right order of magnitude? Would it make sense if it was ten times bigger or smaller?

- Is a geometric mean a sensible choice? For example, when working with different orders of magnitude.

1. What is a bound?

2. What is a geometric mean?

3. What is a Fermi estimate?

4. Give some techniques for making a Fermi estimate.

5. Give upper and lower bounds for the distance driven by a person in the UK each year.

6. How much sugar does a person eat each day?

7. How much time does a person spend asleep in their lifetime?

8. What is population of Paris?

9. How many sausage rolls are sold at a football match?

10. What is the total amount of pocket money given to UK children every year?

PRACTICE QUESTIONS

1. How much more will someone with a degree earn over a lifetime compared to someone whose highest level of qualification is A levels? **[3 marks]**

2. How long would it take one person to read all the books in the local library? **[8 marks]**

3. How long does it take to fill an Olympic swimming pool? **[8 marks]**

4. How much seawater would need to be processed to provide all the salt used by the population of Dubai each day? (Density of seawater = 1.03 g/cm^3) **[6 marks]**

5. How many coffee cups are thrown away every day in the UK? **[3 marks]**

Criticising the Arguments of Others

You need to be able to criticise the arguments of others.

Critical Analysis

Critical analysis is the process of **evaluating** and judging.

You need to be able to identify errors in data, calculations and conclusions and to evaluate whether the results and statements are correct.

This section is about the skills needed to 'unpick' an argument and generally involves questions like the following:
- Is the data correct?
- Where did the data come from?
- Was the data collected correctly (considering sample size or bias)?
- Have the calculations been performed correctly?
- Does the conclusion follow from the facts?
- Are the steps in the argument logical and valid?
- What aspects could be improved?

In critical analysis, questions will concentrate on the analysis of numerical and graphical data, with numerical data usually given in a spreadsheet or tabular form.

In addition to GCSE maths skills, you will be expected to use your knowledge of Analysis of Data (pages 4–19) and Maths for Personal Finance (pages 20–27).

Faulty Data

When collecting data, the way a question is phrased will affect the results obtained.

For example, the following questions are all about government spending on defence (an exaggerated example). Which is likely to provide the best data?
- Should the government spend more money on defence?
- Given the problems with the NHS, should the government spend even more on defence?
- Given the threat of terrorism, should the government spend more money on protecting you?

It is also possible for errors to be introduced when recording the data. Consider the following:

1.67, 1.58, 1.66, 1.70, 1.64, 16.0, 1.62, 1.63

The 16.0 looks suspicious (all other values are given to two decimal places) and is likely to be a mistake in recording the values.

Cause and Effect

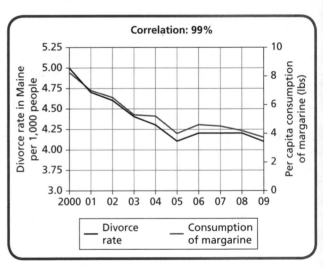

Correlation: 99%

Simply because one value follows another, it does not mean that one causes the other.

Selective Data

Depending on the effect desired, a company could choose to collect or interpret data in the way that serves it best.

Misrepresentation

Data can be misrepresented by only selecting a key section of it. This is like assuming that what somebody wears to an interview is how they dress all the time.

A company might use one section of data to show its products in a good light. For example, to market its shampoo successfully a company could do the following:

1. Give a sample to 100 groups of 10 people.
2. Choose data from the group that reacts most favourably to the product.
3. Advertise using a statement that, 'In a scientific trial, 9 out of 10 people said they preferred Satin Shimmer to their usual brand!'

To collect data, a survey might be conducted where a sample of the population is chosen containing 100 people aged 18–25, 100 aged 26–33, 100 aged 34–41, all the way up to aged 97.

It is good that the sample contains all age groups. However, as the population contains a lot more people aged 18–25 than people aged 90–97, it is a poor representation. A stratified sample would be more appropriate.

Incomplete Data

Information may also be presented in an incomplete form. For example:
28% of people approve of the government's decision.
22% of people disapprove of the government's decision.

Whilst it looks like the majority approve, what about the massive 50% who did not give an opinion or did not even reply to the survey?

Example

During the Second World War, the Americans decided that too many of their planes were being shot down by the Germans and that they should armour them. The problem with armour, however, is that it is heavy and not ideal for planes.

The Americans gathered some statistics and gave the problem to their crack team of mathematicians at the Statistics Research Group:

Section of Plane	Bullet Holes per Square Foot (not real values)
Engine	1.03
Fuel System	1.47
Fuselage	1.68

The officers decided that the best solution would be to protect the planes where they were being hit most, i.e. in the fuselage, but they wanted to check with the experts.

Abraham Wald, an Austrian immigrant, told them that they should not do this – they should armour the engines.

This qualification is all about what is happening 'behind' the numbers, i.e. what they are actually saying.

Wald reasoned that the Americans were counting the number of holes in the planes that *came back* (there could be a lot of holes in the fuselage and the plane would still return) – perhaps the planes that were hit in the engine were simply not coming back!

The Air Force armoured the engines.

SUMMARY

● **When critically analysing data consider the following:**

- ○ Is the data correct?
- ○ Where did the data come from?
- ○ Was the data collected correctly?
- ○ Is it only a small part of the entire data?
- ○ Have the calculations been performed correctly – are there any errors of calculation and is the mathematical technique appropriate in this situation?
- ○ Does the conclusion follow from the facts or is the conclusion based on only the parts that lead to the desired conclusion with other contradictory elements excluded?
- ○ Are the steps in the argument logical and valid – is it reasonable that one thing follows from another?
- ○ What aspects could be improved. If necessary, can it be made clearer, simpler or more accurate?

QUICK TEST

1. What is wrong with the following?

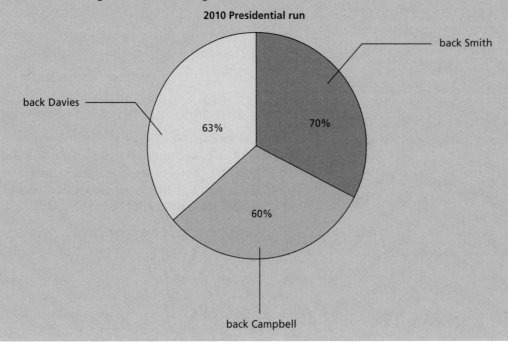

2010 Presidential run

back Smith

back Davies

63%

70%

60%

back Campbell

2. Can both of these representations be correct and, if so, how? What do they say about global warming?

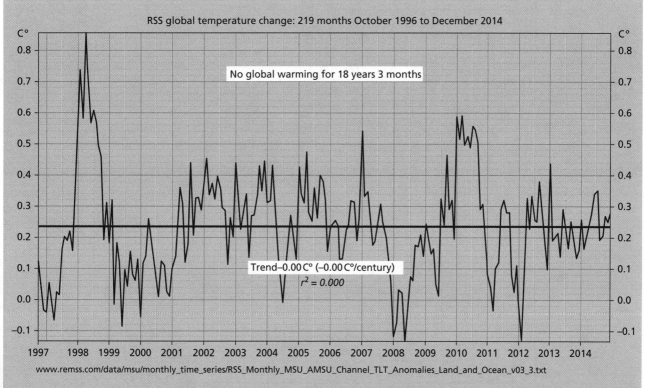

RSS global temperature change: 219 months October 1996 to December 2014

No global warming for 18 years 3 months

Trend–0.00 C° (–0.00 C°/century)
$r^2 = 0.000$

www.remss.com/data/msu/monthly_time_series/RSS_Monthly_MSU_AMSU_Channel_TLT_Anomalies_Land_and_Ocean_v03_3.txt

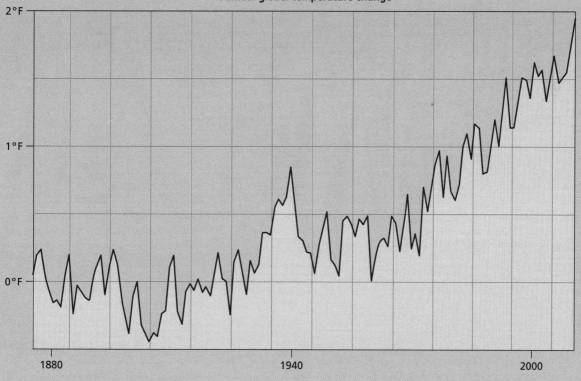

Annual global temperature change

3. Comment on these survey questions and the data they would produce:

    ○ Should your taxes be used to support those not working?

    ○ Do you think the government should help support those who cannot find work?

    ○ What is your opinion on unemployment benefit?

4. In a particular seaside resort, it was found that the number of car accidents throughout the year followed the number of bird attacks. Give possible reasons for this.

5. A section of fence involves a panel of 5 metres and two fence posts. Therefore, for a fence 50 metres long, I would need 10 panels and 20 fences posts. Is this incorrect and, if so, why?

6. This chart represents the frequency of previous Lotto numbers. Which **six** numbers should I choose this week and why?

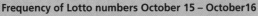

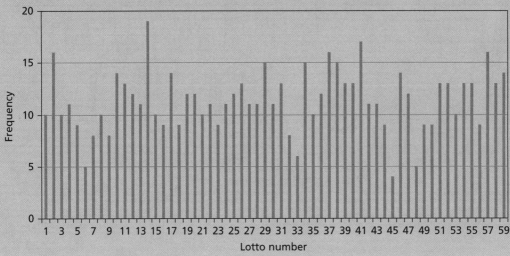

Frequency of Lotto numbers October 15 – October16

PRACTICE QUESTIONS

1. Julio wants to put some money into a savings account at 4% APR.
   He does the following calculation to determine the value after 4 years:

   $0.4 \times 10\,000 = £4\,000$
   $5 \times 4\,000 = £10\,000$

   He notes: This seems a lot – where have I gone wrong?

   Critically analyse Julio's notes and make corrections where necessary.   **[4 marks]**

2. Emanuele buys clothes on sale for £75 after a 20% reduction.
   She thinks that she has saved £15 pounds.
   Her friend was sure she remembered the original price being more than that.

   Criticise the calculations and give the correct original price.   **[3 marks]**

3. Marcus collected some data about the number of takeaways eaten in the last month by
   the 30 students in his class.

Number of Takeaways	Frequency
$0 \leq n < 2$	5
$2 \leq n < 5$	10
$5 \leq n < 8$	9
$8 \leq n < 11$	3

   He carried out the following calculations:

   Mean
   $0 \times 5 + 2 \times 10 + 5 \times 9 + 8 \times 3 = 89$
   $\dfrac{89}{7} = 3.30$

   Median
   3, 5, 9, 10, so median $= \dfrac{5 + 9}{2} = 7$

   Criticise the calculations and give the correct values of mean and median.   **[6 marks]**

4. Jens reads that sales of Mexican food have increased by 275% from 40 million to 110 million,
   but this does not seem quite right to him.

   Explain the likely mistake and give the probable correct value.   **[2 marks]**

5. Mehmet is told that his account will pay 6% AER calculated monthly. He works out that at the
   end of the month his £1000 will have made £5.

   What mistake has he made and what should the correct answer be?   **[4 marks]**

6. Eleanor has a new job with a salary of £45 000.
   She knows that the tax is calculated at 20% on earnings of more than £10 600 and 40%
   on earnings of more than £42 385.
   She works out her tax as follows:

   40% of £42 385 = £16 954
   20% of £10 600 = £2120
   Total tax   = £19 074

   Eleanor thinks that this is a lot.

   Criticise Eleanor's calculations and give the correct value of tax owed.   **[6 marks]**

Summarising and Writing Reports

LEARNING OBJECTIVE

You need to be able to summarise and write reports.

A primary source provides direct or first-hand evidence. These include historical documents, research articles, etc.

Secondary sources describe, discuss, interpret, comment upon, analyse, evaluate, summarise and process primary sources. These include articles in newspapers or popular magazines, book or movie reviews and articles in scholarly journals that discuss or evaluate someone else's original research.

Communicating clear arguments involves:
- valid evidence, preferably from a referenced primary source rather than secondary
- valid reasoning, correct calculations, logical steps
- an appropriate conclusion, summary or result.

In addition to the above, it is important to make sure that any technical writing (which includes communicating mathematical approaches and solutions) is completely clear and unambiguous.

Technical writing must *avoid*:
- **emotive** comments, e.g. *'Continued use of carbon-based fuels is dangerously idiotic for the human race'* – give the facts and, if justified by the evidence, the conclusion and likely outcome
- **vague** comments, e.g. *'A few of the samples were damaged'* – how many or what percentage?
- **contradictory** comments, e.g. *'Although the material shows no discernible performance advantage, it should continue to be banned by the sport'* – either the material assists in performance and should be banned or it does not and should not be banned
- **unjustified** assumptions, e.g. *'Since the introduction of the speed restriction, the number of fatalities has been reduced and, therefore, the restriction should be continued'* – this assumes that the reduction in fatalities is due to the speed restriction but, without further evidence, it could be due to fewer road users, the end of the holiday season, the change from British Summer Time to Greenwich Mean Time, and a lot of other factors.

Example

Yumi wants to work out the best place to set up her ice cream stall.
She tries different positions along the beachfront on different days and puts her results into a table:

	Day 1	Day 2	Day 3	Day 4	Total Unit Sales
Location	west end of promenade	east end of promenade	middle of promenade	on beach itself	
Choc Nice	212	102	244	252	810
Mr Swirly	322	166	298	356	1142
999	301	167	302	334	1104
Lemon Kiss	188	101	233	198	1720
Magic Milk	156	88	155	176	575
Total	1179	624	1232	1316	5351
%	22.03326481	11.66137171	23.02373388	24.59353392	

Yumi must make careful decisions when choosing where to locate her ice cream stall.

Yumi makes the following notes:

It is obvious that from now on I need to set up on the beach and always make sure I have more Mr Swirly than 999.

Yumi has made a number of mistakes:

● She does not need to give the percentages to 10 significant figures.

● It is not 'obvious' that she should set up on the beach – she has no record of the weather, the time she spent in each place, the day of the week or any other factors that could affect sales.

● She did not always sell more Mr Swirly than 999.

● The two totals horizontally and vertically do not match up.

● The horizontal total for Lemon Kiss seems wrong as she consistently sold less of these than the 999.

● There is no indication of what the percentage refers to.

Yumi could improve her data by including:

● prices

● weather information, e.g. temperature, whether it is sunny, etc.

● time of year (if it is holiday season she might expect to sell more)

● day of the week (if days 3 and 4 were at the weekend, she might expect to sell more, wherever she is)

● time spent at each location, start time and finish time (time of day might affect sales).

SUMMARY

● **Check that the information is valid.**

● **Check that it is consistent and reasonable – are there any values that do not seem to fit with the others?**

● **Check that the writing avoids emotive, vague, contradictory and unjustified comments.**

● **Check that conclusions justified – is more information needed?**

QUICK TEST

1. What is valid evidence?

2. What is the difference between a primary and secondary sources of information?

3. State **three** things to avoid when writing a report.

4. What is wrong with using this formula to calculate an average in a spread sheet: =E1+E2+E3/3?

5. Ice cream sales correlate with bikini sales.
    Why is it not valid reasoning to say that ice cream sales cause bikini sales?

6. *'Henry smokes 20 cigarettes a day and there is absolutely nothing wrong with him.'*
    What comments could you make about this report?

7. *'When I visited Paris, I was surprised by how many French people spoke perfect English.'*
    Is this a fair report? Explain your answer.

8. *'Being a 'grammar Nazi' could mean you're an introvert. If you're one of those people who just can't let incorrect use of grammar lie, then you might be someone who takes more pleasure in solitude than others, according to a study.'*
    What is the key element of this headline?

PRACTICE QUESTIONS

1. Marie was asked to write a short report on whether her school library should replace printed books with e-books. She asked the 30 students in her class and wrote the following:

8 students wanted e-books, 4 students wanted to keep printed books and 19 students had no opinion. As the number who wanted e-books was a massive 100% more than those wanting to keep printed books, there is a clear desire to change and I think we should go ahead.

Analyse Marie's report. Identify any errors and suggest improvements.　　　　　　**[4 marks]**

2. Baobao was asked compile a report about the TV viewing habits of adolescents. She produced the following report.

To study the amount of TV watched by adolescents, I asked 90 students in my year and here are my results.

Hours	TV	Other Screens
1	3	1
2	24	11
3	26	20
4	16	40
5	10	18
6	5	10

Mean number of hours $= \dfrac{(4 \times 1) + (25 \times 2) + (46 \times 3) + (56 \times 4) + (28 \times 5) + (15 \times 6)}{90} = 7.18$ hours

Analyse Baobao's report. Identify any errors and suggest improvements.　　　　　　**[6 marks]**

3. Habib conducted a survey and wrote a report on his findings.

I asked 120 people, 80 men and 40 women, in the town about which films they preferred. They scored the films out of 10 and then I worked out an average for each cell.

	Star Wars – A New Beginning	Me Before You	Totals
Men	5.6	5.0	5.3
Women	6.2	5.6	5.9
Totals	5.9	5.3	5.6

I was surprised, because generally women prefer love films, not action films.

Correct any mistakes and write a short, improved report on the findings.　　　　　　**[8 marks]**

Critical Analysis

LEARNING OBJECTIVES

You need to be able to:

● compare results from a model with real data

● critically analyse data quoted in the media, political campaigns, marketing, etc.

Criticising a Model

With any model there are always assumptions and simplifications. You must be able to recognise what these are and the effect they have on the outcomes.

Example

James wants to raise money for charity at his local fête. He decides to set up a stall where you have to throw a ball into a jar to win a prize.

He asks everyone he knows to have a go and concludes that the probability of success is 20%. He decides that he will charge £1 for two throws and buy prizes for 50p each.

He expects to make an average of 40p per go.

What could be the problems with his model?

Depending on who James asked, he could have overestimated or (more seriously, for his money making) underestimated the probability.

Secondly, he has assumed that the throws are **independent**. Someone could have several goes and develop the expertise to succeed, allowing them to win every time (although, even in the worst case scenario, he would not lose money).

Misleading Representation

Graphical Representations

By choosing a small section of a scale, quantities can appear to grow dramatically on a graph or one quantity can appear much larger than another. In the graph, sales have only grown from 240 000 to 240 630, i.e. by 0.26% – hardly 'massive', as stated in the headline.

Massive Growth in Newspaper Sales!

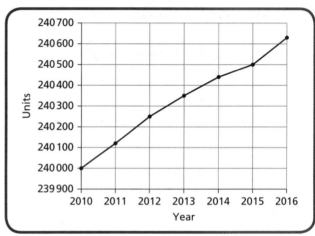

Using two- or three-dimensional representations can also give a false indication of quantities.

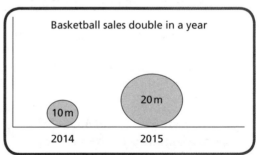

Because the area of the circle increases by a factor of 4 (2^2) when the height doubles, the 2015 sales appear much more than twice those of 2014.

Media Statements

It is important to be able to analyse the reasoning behind media headlines. Newspapers in particular use emotive language to attract attention.

Consider the following headlines:

Massive increase in road deaths in town centre! Increase of 33% since last year!

If there were only three deaths last year, an increase to four would not be exceptional and would be within the expected annual variation. How likely is it that there would be exactly the same number as last year?

People who use talcum powder are 40% more likely to have cancer!

In this headline, the writer has deliberated used relative risk instead of absolute risk.

The overall probability of an individual having this type of cancer was 10 in 100 000 (0.0001). The study indicated that regular use of talcum powder would increase this risk to 14 in 100 000 (0.00014). This is still a low risk, but it has increased relatively by 40%, which makes a much more exciting headline for the newspaper.

SUMMARY

● **It is important to:**

○ **analyse all the assumptions**

○ **check how the information has been presented**

○ **think about the intended purpose and check whether only favourable information is used.**

QUICK TEST

1. *'Man tossing coin gets 20 heads in a row!'* Why might this not be exceptional?

2. *'8 out of 10 owners said their cats preferred it.'* What questions should be asked of this data?

3. Comment on the following: *'Driving in daylight is more dangerous than driving in fog.'*

4. *'I sold 320 ice creams today and I am sure I will sell the same tomorrow.'* Is this comment sensible?

5. Because of the increase in the number of horse-drawn carriages on the streets in 1894, *The Times* newspaper predicted: *'In 50 years, every street in London will be buried under nine feet of manure.'* What were they assuming?

6. How could the following be improved:

$41 billion in sales

$4.1 billion in sales

$4.3 billion in sales

$8 billion in sales

$8.2 billion in sales

GDP of Afghanistan $21 billion

$11.3 billion in sales

$9.4 billion in sales

Billions of dollars

COOL DAWGS

PRACTICE QUESTION

1. The *Daily Record* reported on the election with this report:

Massive Mandate for National Party
The National Party has increased its lead by more than 50% as the country endorses their anti-immigration and austerity policies.

2012 Election

Party	Number of Votes (Millions)
National Party	20.7
Democratic Party	8.5
Worker Party	19.8
Green Party	3.0
Others	7.1

2016 Election

Party	Number of Votes (Millions)
National Party	20.5
Democratic Party	14.3
Worker Party	19.1
Green Party	6.1
Others	12.8

a) The leader of the Green Party contacted the newspaper to complain about the representation of the results.

Was she justified? **[3 marks]**

b) The leader of the Democratic Party said, '*We had the biggest increase of any party and this shows the country's disgust with the offensive racist ideas of the National Party.*'

Comment on whether it is possible to justify this from the data. **[3 marks]**

c) The leader of one of the smaller parties stated, '*The results show the huge level of discontent in the country as they have voted against this government.*'

Comment on this and show working to justify your answers. **[3 marks]**

The Normal Distribution

LEARNING OBJECTIVES

You need to be able to:

- recall the properties of normal distribution and use notation to describe a normal distribution in terms of mean and standard deviation
- use a calculator or tables to find probabilities for normally distributed data.

Knowledge of normal distribution will help with the following types of question:

- What proportion of the population can comfortably walk through a standard door of height 1981 mm?
- What is the chance that a washing machine will last ten years without needing repair?
- Why is birth weight not normally distributed?

Properties of the Normal Distribution

Normal distribution means that:

- the mean, median and mode of a data set are equal
- the data produces a 'bell' shaped curve that is symmetrical about the mean (μ)
- the area under the curve represents probability and is equal to one
- the normal curve approaches, but never touches, the x-axis as it extends away from the mean.

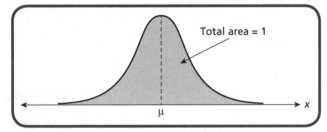

Notation

Notation uses symbols to represent the values in a series.

If a variable Z has a normal distribution, then: $Z \sim N(\mu, \sigma^2)$

Where:

- N means it belongs to a normal distribution
- μ is the mean
- σ is the **standard deviation**.

For standard normal distribution: $Z \sim N(\mu, 1)$

Where:

- Mean (μ) = 0
- Standard deviation (σ) = 1
- All scores are relative to μ and σ.

Approximately 68% ($\frac{2}{3}$) of observations lie within one standard deviation of the mean and 95% lie within two standard deviations of the mean.

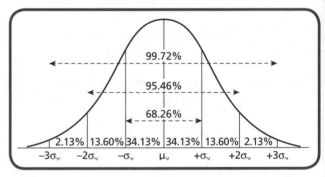

Example

Suppose the life expectancy of a microwave (M) is normally distributed with a mean life span of 9 years and a standard deviation of 2 years.

$M \sim N(9, 2^2)$

- 68.26% of microwaves would be expected to last between 7 and 11 years (one standard deviation).
- 95.46% would last between 5 and 13 years (two standard deviations).

If a microwave stops working at 4 years, would there be a case against the manufacturer?

Possibly, as only 2.5% of microwaves would be expected to fail before 5 years.

Calculating Probabilities

All real life normal distributions can be **standardised** by relating a random variable to a standard mean of zero.

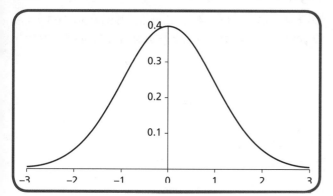

1. Draw a picture of the situation. What part of the graph is required?

2. Standardise the normally distributed variable (Z) by relating it to z using the formula:
$$z = \frac{Z - \mu}{\sigma}$$

3. Use Table 1: Normal Distribution Function (on page 146) or a calculator to obtain the probabilities.

4. Relate back to the context.

The tables only provide for the positive half of the distribution (to the right of μ). You must use symmetry to find the negative half.

Reading the Tables

The full tables are given on pages 146–147 and will be made available to you in the exam.

Table 1 – Normal Distribution Function
The table gives the probability (p) that a normally distributed random variable (Z), with mean = 0 and variance = 1, is less than or equal to z.

Read down the z column to find the first decimal place and then across to the appropriate column for the second decimal place.

The shows the probability for a z **score** of 0.43 = 0.66640, i.e. 66.64% of the data lies below or before this.

z	0.00	0.01	0.02	0.03	0.04	0.05
0.0	0.50000	0.50399	0.50798	0.51197	0.51595	0.51994
0.1	0.53983	0.54380	0.54776	0.55172	0.55567	0.55962
0.2	0.57926	0.58317	0.58706	0.59095	0.59483	0.59871
0.3	0.61791	0.62172	0.62552	0.62930	0.63307	0.63683
0.4	0.65542	0.65910	0.66276	0.66640	0.67003	0.67364
0.5	0.69146	0.69497	0.69847	0.70194	0.70540	0.70884

To find the z score, use Table 2: Percentage Points of the Normal Distribution (on page 147).

Table 2 – Percentage Points of the Normal Distribution
The table gives the values of z satisfying $P(Z \le z) = p$, where Z is the normally distributed random variable with mean = 0 and variance = 1.

Read down the p column to find the first decimal place and across to the appropriate column for the second decimal place.

The example shows that for a probability of 0.85, the z score is 1.0364 (or 1.0364 standard deviations right of the mean).

p	0.00	0.01	0.02	0.03	0.04	0.05	0.06
0.5	0.0000	0.0251	0.0502	0.0753	0.1004	0.1257	0.1510
0.6	0.2533	0.2793	0.3055	0.3319	0.3585	0.3853	0.4125
0.7	0.5244	0.5534	0.5828	0.6128	0.6433	0.6745	0.7063
0.8	0.8416	0.8779	0.9154	0.9542	0.9945	1.0364	1.0803
0.9	1.2816	1.3408	1.4051	1.4758	1.5548	1.6449	1.7507

Example
Returning to the microwave example:
What is the probability of a microwave failing before 4 years?

1. Sketch the situation showing the required part of curve:

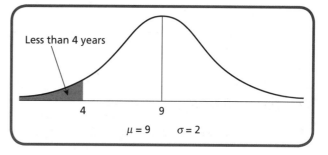

2. This gives: $z = \dfrac{4-9}{z} - 2.5$

3. From Table 1 (using symmetry):

$P(Z \le -2.5) = 1 - P(Z \le 2.5)$
$= 1 - 0.99379$
$= 0.00621$
$= 0.621\%$

4. In other words, there is less than a 1% chance of the microwave failing within 4 years.

This may appear quite low, but if there were 2 million microwaves sold, then 0.00621×2 million $= 12\,420$ expected failures before 4 years.

Example

For the microwave example, where would the middle 50% of the data lie?

The positive side of the curve suggests that up to Z_2 would be 75% or 0.75

If $P\left(z \le \dfrac{z-\mu}{\sigma}\right) \le 0.75$, then $z = 0.6745$ (from Table 2)

So if $z = \dfrac{z-9}{2}$

$0.6745 = \dfrac{z-9}{2}$

$Z = 10.349$ on the positive side and 7.651 on the negative side $(9 - 1.349)$

So, the middle 50% of the data lies between 7.65 years (7 years 8 months) and 10.349 years (10 years 4 months).

SUMMARY

- The normal distribution is common and has specific properties.
- 68%, 96% and 99.7% of observations lie within one, two or three standard deviations (σ).
- Notation is $Z \sim N(\mu, \sigma^2)$
- All real variables can be standardised via the z score: $z = \dfrac{z-\mu}{\sigma}$
- Always try to relate back to the original context.
- Table 1 helps with reading probabilities for z scores.
- Table 2 allows probabilities to become z scores.

QUICK TEST

1. Give **four** properties of the normal distribution?

2. What proportion of normally distributed data lies within one standard deviation?

3. Write the Greek letter normally used to represent the mean?

4. How is a real life variable standardised?

5. Explain why it is not possible to find (directly) negative z scores on Table 1: The Normal Distribution Function?

6. Using the tables, what is $P(Z \le 1.9876)$?

7. Find the probability of $P(Z \ge 1.9876)$.

8. If a z score has a probability of 63.34%, what is the z score?

PRACTICE QUESTIONS

1. A company pays its employees a mean wage of £14.42 an hour with a standard deviation of £2.66

   If the wages are normally distributed, determine:

   a) the proportion of the workers getting wages between £11.88 and £16.05 an hour.   **[5 marks]**

   b) the minimum wage of the highest paid 5%.   **[3 marks]**

2. A standard internal door has a height of 1981 mm.

   The mean height of a male in the UK is 177.8 cm with a standard deviation of 10.16 cm.

   What proportion of males would be expected not to be able to walk comfortably
   (without bending down) through a doorway of this height?   **[3 marks]**

3. The mean length of 100 parts produced by a lathe is 20.05 mm with a standard deviation of 0.02 mm.

   Find the probability that a part selected at random would have a length:

   a) between 20.03 mm and 20.07 mm   **[2 marks]**

   b) between 20.06 mm and 20.07 mm   **[2 marks]**

   c) less than 20.01 mm   **[2 marks]**

   d) greater than 20.09 mm.   **[1 mark]**

Population and Sample

You need to be able to:

- understand how a simple random sample is used to represent a population
- calculate the mean or a point estimate of a sample.

Probabilities and Estimation

How many disease-causing microorganisms are needed to achieve some understanding of the behaviour of the entire disease at a particular stage of infection?

If the whole **population** of microorganisms is required, then it is an impossible task to find a cure. Often, only a **sample** is available and inferences from this sample could be crucial.

The sample represents the population and the characteristics shown by that sample hopefully replicate what is going on in the population as a whole.

Where such occurrences have a **normal distribution, confidence intervals** can also be used.

Population and Sample

This follows on from Analysis of Data on pages 4–19.

Type	Population	Sample	Random Sample
Definition	The entire number of members or objects under consideration	A subset of the population	Each item or member has an equal chance of being selected
Examples	Blades of grass in a field; number of polar bears in the wild; light bulbs in production in the UK; members list of a club or community	Number of blades in 1 square metre; number of polar bears in certain area; light bulbs produced by one factory in one day; all male members	Random procedures are used, e.g. – names from a hat – throwing a dice – tossing a coin – random number generator
Pros	Captures all aspects of the members – all inclusive	Easier to count or consider; less time consuming; cheaper	Should be unbiased and representative of the whole population
Cons	Can be difficult to count or consider, e.g. blades of grass	May not be representative; bias needs to be avoided	Care needed to avoid bias; possibly time consuming for stratified random sampling

Generally it is easier to consider a sample rather than the entire population. However, it is important that the sample is representative of the population.

Take the cases of the polling carried out before both the EU Referendum and the US Presidential election of 2016. Pollsters seem to have got this very wrong and there are genuine concerns about why and how this occurred. Were the polls representative or did some individuals that were surveyed hide their true allegiances?

Example
A survey is to be carried out at a school to find out views on the canteen food.

A random stratified sample could be carried out to include all years and maintain gender proportions. However, not all of those chosen would be 100% cooperative. Some may be more interested in 'winding up' the questioner and give false information. This means that the results cannot be truly trusted. How could this be improved?

In such cases, the bigger the sample the better. However, care is still needed in the way the survey is carried out. Ultimately no survey or questionnaire is perfect and whilst it may be representative it does not always give the whole picture.

Mean of a Sample and Point Estimate

A **statistic** is a calculated numerical value that represents an aspect of the population data.

An important statistic often used to highlight the behaviour of the population is the **sample mean ($\bar{x}$)**.

A **point estimate** uses a sample statistic (e.g. the sample mean at a point to represent the population.

As the population data and the population mean (μ) may be difficult to obtain, a point estimate provides a way of interpreting the sample data in relation to the population. In short, this can be seen as quality control.

Remember that the bigger the sample, the more representative and reliable the point estimate.

Population Mean (μ)	$\dfrac{\text{The sum of all population data points}}{\text{Total of the population}}$	For example, the number of children per woman in the UK
Sample Mean ($\bar{x}$)	$\bar{x} = \dfrac{\sum x}{n}$	For example, the number of children per woman in London

Example
In a study to find out how many hours a week students spend on the internet, six different samples are taken. The sample means are:

10.33   11.25   12.05   10.74   11.78   11.02

How could these sample means be used to estimate a mean for the population?

This depends on the level of detail around the sample means.

If more information was available regarding the number of students in each sample, then it would be possible to calculate a mean for all (total) students within these six samples.

For example, if there were 10 students in each sample, then the total of all the samples would be 60 and the collective mean can be calculated as:

$$\bar{x} = \frac{(10.33 + 11.25 + 12.05 + 10.74 + 11.78 + 11.02) \times 10}{60}$$
$$= 11.195$$

If the collective sample means were as above, 11.195 could be used as a point estimate for the population.

However, the six samples might not represent the population in an unbiased way and if the sample sizes were larger they could be more trusted.

SUMMARY

- Populations can vary and are very often difficult to fully count or survey.
- Samples are often used to represent the population, but there are pros and cons.
- A sample should preferably be random (to avoid bias) and represent all the different aspects of the population.
- Surveys and questionnaires can be difficult to carry out perfectly and responses may need further analysis to assess whether they provide a true representation.
- Point estimates, such as the sample mean, can be used to represent the population.
- The larger the sample size, the more reliable the estimate.

QUICK TEST

1. What is a sample mean?
2. Explain what 'population' means.
3. What is a point estimate?
4. What is the difference between a population and a sample?
5. Why is best to alleviate bias in a sample?
6. Why might a survey be biased?
7. What impact does sample size have on the sample mean?

PRACTICE QUESTIONS

1. A sample of 10 similar solar panels are weighed (kg):

19.55	20.51	20.59	19.31	19.18	20.52	20.04	20.19	20.83	20.67

a) Calculate the sample mean. [2 marks]

b) Another random sample of 15 panels has a sample mean of 19.758.

Calculate the mean for all 25 solar panels. [2 marks]

c) Which of the sample means would best represent the population and why? [1 mark]

2. The labels on bottles of drink state that the volume of contents is 330 ml.

The actual contents are set so that the volume of drink is distributed normally with a mean average of 340 ml and a standard deviation of 3 ml.

a) What is the probability that a randomly selected bottle contains less than advertised? [5 marks]

b) Comment on the likelihood of a complaint. [2 marks]

Confidence Intervals

Calculating Confidence Intervals

If a population (of data) is normally distributed (see pages 56–59) then:

$Z \sim N(\mu, \sigma^2)$
i.e. Z belongs to a normal distribution with parameters μ and σ^2.

If a sample of that population is also normally distributed, then any possible sample mean is also normally distributed, so:

$$\bar{x} \sim N\left(\mu, \frac{\sigma^2}{\mu}\right)$$

Where:

● μ is the population mean
● σ is the population standard deviation
● n is the number of data points in the sample
● the sample standard deviation is $\frac{\sigma}{\sqrt{n}}$ and for
samples $z = \dfrac{\bar{x} - \mu}{\frac{\sigma}{\sqrt{n}}}$

General Example for a 95% Confidence Interval

A 95% interval is often used but the larger the confidence interval, the less precise the estimate ($\bar{x}$).

An 80% interval would imply a more precise estimate – generally the true value (μ) would lie in 80 out of 100 samples. However, a 95% interval allows for more confidence that μ is within the interval.

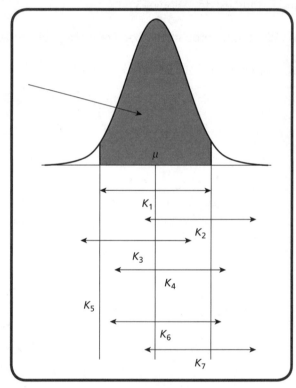

95% of all sample means ($\bar{x}$) should be within the dotted lines either side of μ.

Notice that if the sample mean is outside the dotted line, the interval will not contain μ.

Samples of the same size have the same standard error, so the 95% width is the same for all of them.

So, for a 95% confidence interval:

$$P\left(-1.96 \le \frac{\bar{x} - \mu}{\frac{\sigma}{\sqrt{n}}} \le 1.96\right) = 0.95$$

Example

The mean weight (μ) of solar panels is unknown but the variance is 0.38

Use the following sample of 10 weights to calculate a 95% confidence interval.

| 19.55 | 20.51 | 20.59 | 19.31 | 19.18 | 20.52 | 20.04 | 20.19 | 20.83 | 20.67 |

$n = 10$, $\bar{x} = 20.139$ and $\sigma^2 = 0.38$, so $\sigma = \sqrt{0.38} = 0.6124$

$$
\begin{aligned}
\text{Interval} \quad &= (\bar{x} - 1.96\,\tfrac{\sigma}{\sqrt{n}}, \bar{x} + 1.96\,\tfrac{\sigma}{\sqrt{n}}) \\
&= (20.139 - 1.96 \times \tfrac{0.6124}{\sqrt{10}}, 20.139 + 1.96 \times \tfrac{0.6124}{\sqrt{10}}) \\
&= (20.139 - 0.38, 20.139 + 0.38) \\
&= (19.76, 20.52)
\end{aligned}
$$

⬤ For a 99% interval use (−2.58, 2.58) as given within the tables on pages 146–147.
⬤ For 95% use (−1.96, 1.96).
⬤ For 90% use (−1.64, 1.64).

So there is a 95% confidence that the population mean lies between 19.76 kg and 20.52 kg.

The average is normally quoted as 20 kg, so this seems in line with expectations.

Example

A biologist studies a species of caterpillar and weighs a random sample of 20.

The weights are known to be normally distributed with a standard deviation of 0.2

The weights are as follows:

5.2, 5.5, 4.5, 5.7, 5.4, 5.5, 5.5, 5.1, 5.1, 5, 5.2, 5, 6, 5.2, 5.4, 5.8, 6, 5.9, 5.3, 5.2

Using these values, find a 95% confidence interval for the mean weight of caterpillars surveyed.

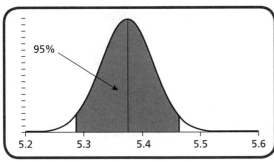

$n = 20$, $\bar{x} = 5.375$ and $\sigma = 0.2$

$$
\begin{aligned}
\text{Interval} \quad &= (\bar{x} - 1.96\,\tfrac{\sigma}{\sqrt{n}}, \bar{x} + 1.96\,\tfrac{\sigma}{\sqrt{n}}) \\
&= (5.375 - 1.96 \times \tfrac{0.2}{\sqrt{20}}, 5.375 + 1.96 \times \tfrac{0.2}{\sqrt{20}}) \\
&= (5.375 - 0.088, 5.375 + 0.088) \\
&= (5.287, 5.463)
\end{aligned}
$$

Example

The volume of vegetable oil in 43 identical containers is measured in litres.
The following statistics are calculated from the results:
$\bar{x} = 10.19$ and $\sigma = 0.13758$

a) Stating a necessary assumption about the 43 containers, construct a 90% confidence interval for the mean volume of vegetable oil, giving the limits to two decimal places.

Assumption is that the 43 containers are a random sample.

Interval $= 10.19 \pm (1.64 \times \dfrac{0.13758}{\sqrt{43}})$

So, the interval is between 10.16 and 10.22 litres.

b) Labels on the containers indicate a volume of 10 litres of vegetable oil.
Comment on the likely accuracy of this labelling.

10 is outside the confidence interval range, which suggests the mean is greater than 10.
This probably means consumers will be less likely to complain but there are extra costs for the manufacturer.

Example

A sample of 20 means where recorded for the weight of a particular object and a 95% confidence interval calculated.

Approximately how many of the sample means would be expected not to contain the population mean?

95% would be expected, so 5% of 20 = 1

SUMMARY

- A confidence interval is the interval within which an unknown parameter of distribution (usually μ) is expected to lie with a given level of confidence.

- In the exam, confidence intervals will always be symmetrical and the sample size and confidence level will be given.

- The sample mean distribution is also normal and $\bar{x} \sim N(\mu, \frac{\sigma^2}{n})$. Use $z = \dfrac{\bar{x} - \mu}{\frac{\sigma}{\sqrt{n}}}$.

- Typical confidence intervals are 90%, 95% or 99%, but any can be found.

- To calculate these intervals use $(\bar{x} \pm 1.64 \frac{\sigma}{\sqrt{n}})$, $(\bar{x} \pm 1.96 \frac{\sigma}{\sqrt{n}})$ and $(\bar{x} \pm 1.96 \frac{\sigma}{\sqrt{n}})$, respectively.

- The wider the interval, the more likely the population mean is included.

- Relate solutions back to the context for true understanding.

QUICK TEST

1. Define what is meant by a confidence interval?

2. How is a sample that is normally distributed usually denoted?

3. How is the sample standard deviation calculated?

4. Give examples of confidence intervals that are regularly used.

5. What is the general formula for finding a 90% confidence interval?

PRACTICE QUESTIONS

1. A random sample of 32 was taken from a normally distributed population.
The value of the sample mean ($\bar{x}$) is 15.64

    a) Using these values, find a 99% confidence interval for μ.   **[3 marks]**

    b) It is believed that the value of μ is 18.3

        Use your confidence interval to comment on this.   **[1 mark]**

2. The director of Juicy Jams states, *'On average the contents of our jars of jam weigh more than all of our competitors.'*
The weights of the contents of Juicy Jams' jars are distributed with mean μ and a variance of 39.
The following weights represent a random sample of Juicy Jams' jars:

    186 g   176 g   185 g   186 g   174 g   179 g   184 g   174 g   186 g   188 g

The mean weight of the contents of similar jam jars is 176.9 g.

Calculate a 95% confidence interval for μ for the contents of Juicy Jams' jars.
Hence comment on the statement from the director.   **[6 marks]**

3. A random sample of 10 test results for a maths class has a total of 69 marks.
The results are normally distributed with a standard deviation of 4.

Find an 80% confidence interval for the population mean.
Comment on your results.   **[4 marks]**

4. A random sample with a mean of 80 is chosen from a normal distribution with a variance of 29 where the
mean μ is unknown.
The 90% confidence interval is calculated as (77.719867, 82.80133).

What was the size of the sample?   **[4 marks]**

5. The lifetimes, in hours, of 100 NRG light bulbs is recorded, giving the summary data:
$n = 100$, $\Sigma x = 10774$, $\Sigma x^2 = 1736695$

Assuming the 100 bulbs are a random sample, find a 99% confidence interval for the mean lifetime of
NRG light bulbs.
(Use the sample standard deviation (s) to represent σ).   **[4 marks]**

Correlation and Regression

This topic builds on the association of two variables (see pages 6–9) and a general understanding of negative and positive correlation where measures are given between –1 and 1.

Correlation

When constructing a **line of best fit**, the mean of the x and y variables $(\bar{x}, \bar{y})$ needs to be on the line.

Using $(\bar{x}, \bar{y})$ as a reference point can also show an indication of correlation:

Positive Correlation
Most data points are in the 3rd and 1st quadrant relative to $(\bar{x}, \bar{y})$.

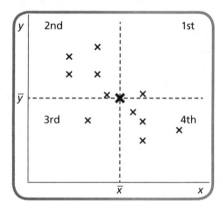

No Correlation
Data points are scattered with no obvious pattern relative to $(\bar{x}, \bar{y})$.

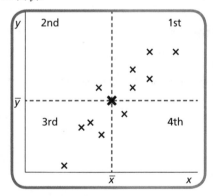

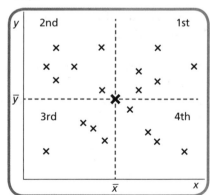

Negative Correlation
Most data points are in the 2nd and 4th quadrant relative to $(\bar{x}, \bar{y})$.

If $(\bar{x}, \bar{y})$ is considered in the same way as the origin, then:

- the 1st quadrant will have positive deviations from the mean for x and y data
- the 3rd quadrant will only have negative deviations.

As the product of a positive multiplied by a positive or a negative multiplied by a negative is always positive, it helps explain a positive correlation.

The same logic can be used for a negative correlation or no correlation.

Formula for Correlation Coefficient (r)

From this general idea, the deviations (distances) from the mean are used to create the formula for a linear correlation coefficient:

$$r = \frac{S_{xy}}{\sqrt{S_{xx}S_{yy}}} = \frac{\sum xy - \dfrac{\sum x \sum y}{n}}{\sqrt{(\sum x^2 - \dfrac{(\sum x)^2}{n})(\sum y^2 - \dfrac{\sum(y)^2}{n})}}$$

Where S_{xy}, S_{xx} and S_{yy} are measures of sums and differences of the mean and individual x and y variables.

There is no need to remember the formula – it is what calculators use to provide the **product moment correlation coefficient (pmcc)**.

It is more crucial to be able to interpret what the pmcc might imply.

The Product Moment Correlation Coefficient

The pmcc gives the strength of a correlation and always has a value in the range of −1 to 1:

- When $r = -1$, there is a perfect negative correlation.
- When $r = +1$, there is a perfect positive correlation.

The pmcc formula will confirm that in both cases the data points lie on a straight line. This might strongly suggest a relationship or causation, but this should not just be assumed.

Other r-values will need to be considered in context, e.g. although a value of $r = 0.8$ might seem strong, does it make sense in context?

- When $r = 0$, there is no linear correlation but there could be other non-linear correlations.

Example

Interpret the meaning of the two data sets below, which have a correlation coefficient of zero.

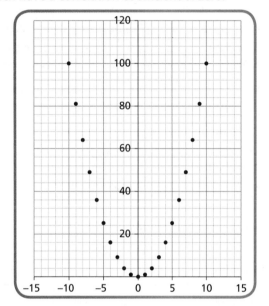

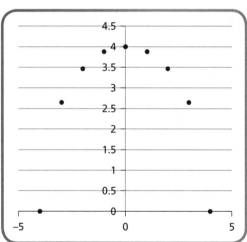

There is clearly no linear correlation, yet there is another non-linear correlation.

Further investigation would be required (which is beyond this course).

DAY 7

Regression Lines

Drawing the line of best fit to include the $(\bar{x}, \bar{y})$ helps estimate the equation of the line of best fit using $y = mx + c$, finding the gradient m ($\frac{\text{change in } y}{\text{change in } x}$) and c (the y-intercept).

However, there is a more mathematical way of obtaining the equation of the line of best fit – using a **regression line**.

This method basically considers the vertical deviations from all possible lines of best fit so as to reduce the sum of the squares of these deviations to its minimum.

You do not need to know how this works (for this course). However, you do need to be able to:

● calculate the equation of a regression line using a calculator
● plot a regression line from its equation
● use interpolation with regression lines to make predictions.

The equation of a regression line is in the form $y = a + bx$.

Some calculators may give the equation in a slightly different form, e.g. $y = mx + c$. This can be rearranged to $y = c + mx$, then change the c and m to $y = a + bx$

Interpretation
There are two important aspects that need interpretation for linear equations:

● b – this is the **gradient** and essentially tells how much the y variable increases for every unit increase of the x variable
● a – this is the y-intercept and gives a value for y when x is zero.

Interpolation is when estimates occur within the data set range.

Extrapolation is to assume that the trend continues outside the data range.

Example
A second-hand car dealership has 10 cars for sale.

They decide to investigate the link between the age of the cars, x years, and the mileage, y (thousand miles):

Age (years) x	5	3.5	6	2.5	6	5	6	3.5	2.5	5
Mileage (1000) y	25	23	46	26	42	49	23	29	27	32

Use a calculator to answer the following.

a) Find the equation of the line of best fit.

From the calculator: $b = 3.5143$ and $c = 16.386$

Equation of line: $y = 16.386 + 3.5143x$

b) What do the values of b and a suggest?

b – for every year added, mileage increase by 3.5143 thousand miles

c – a car zero years old has travelled 16.386 thousand miles (this is not sensible)

c) What is the correlation coefficient r?

$r = 0.4996899$, so 0.5

d) What does the value of r suggest?

A positive but weak correlation.

e) Estimate the mileage covered by cars over:

i) 4 years

$y = 16.386 + (3.5143 \times 4) = 30.4432$ thousand miles

ii) 9 years

$y = 16.386 + (3.5143 \times 9) = 48.0147$ thousand miles

f) State which of **e)** is more reliable and why?

The value for 4 years is more reliable (interpolation) – 9 years is outside the data range (extrapolating).

g) Does it matter that the y units are in 1000s?

No, scaling does not affect correlation or regression.

h) Comment on the findings and how the investigation could be improved.

Low correlation questions the validity of causation and the line of regression. Other factors, such as location and main use of vehicle, could affect mileage. Increasing the data size could improve validity.

- The correlation coefficient is r (calculated by a calculator as $r = \dfrac{S_{xy}}{\sqrt{S_{xx}S_{yy}}}$).

- If $r = \pm 1$, all the points lie on a straight line, which suggests causation. However, be cautious – other values for r need considering in context.

- The equation for a regression line is $y = a + bx$ (from $y = mx + c$) in calculator form, where a gives the value for y when $x = 0$, and b gives the change in y for every unit change in x.

- Calculator technique and use is crucial.

- Interpretation is essential, remembering:
  - interpolation (inside the data range)
  - extrapolation (outside the data range)
  - scaling the data has no effect.

QUICK TEST

1. What is the letter used to denote the correlation coefficient?

2. What point is always on the line of best fit and used to consider correlation?

3. What do the a and b values in the regression line equation stand for?

4. Does a correlation coefficient of +1 demonstrate causation?

5. What is the value of y for the regression line $y = 16 + 3.5x$ if $x = 5$?

6. If the original x values are in thousands, what might a sensible scaling be and would this affect the correlation or regression line?

7. If all the data values for x lie between 100 and 200, is it sensible to consider potential y values using a value for x outside this range?

8. Here is some data:

   (96, 79) (84, 93) (75, 73) (93, 85) (85, 82) (90, 94) (72, 74)

   a) Using a calculator to work out the correlation coefficient and comment on the value.

   b) Find the equation of the regression line for the data.

   c) What does the y-intercept value suggest and is this sensible?

DAY 7

PRACTICE QUESTIONS

1. The table contains data concerning five households selected at random from a certain town.

Number of People in Household	2	3	2	4	5
Number of Cars Belonging to Household	1	1	3	1	4

a) Calculate the product moment correlation coefficient (pmcc), r, for the data in the table. **[1 mark]**

b) Give a reason why it would not be sensible to use your answer to draw a conclusion about all the households in the town. **[1 mark]**

2. A city council attempted to reduce traffic congestion by introducing a congestion charge.

The charge was set at £5 for the first year and was then increased by £3 per year.

For each of the first eight years, the council recorded the average number of vehicles entering the city centre each day. The results are shown in the table:

Charge £x	5	8	11	14	17	20	23	26
Average Number, y million	2.3	2.4	2.2	2.2	1.9	1.8	1.8	1.5

a) Work out the correlation coefficient and the equation of the regression line. **[3 marks]**

b) Interpret and comment on the values found for part **a)**. **[3 marks]**

3. Data was recorded about ten apartments in a city.

The graph shows the distance from the city centre and the monthly rent of each apartment.

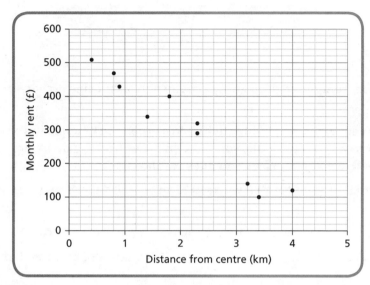

a) Work out the equation of the regression line using the table below to help.
   The first data point is shown. **[3 marks]**

Distance (km)	0.4									
Rent (£)	510									

b) Plot the regression line on the scatter diagram. **[3 marks]**

c) Using the information obtained, what is a good estimate of the rent for an apartment 3 km from the city centre? **[2 marks]**

d) Comment on the usefulness of the regression line in this context. **[2 marks]**

Compound Projects

LEARNING OBJECTIVES

You need to:

● **be able to represent compound projects by activity networks using activity-on-node representation**

● **make sure there is enough time for all activities in a project to happen and ensure they happen in the most efficient way, for example, you could put your trousers on before your socks, or vice versa, but you need to do both before you put your shoes on**

● **identify the activities in a project that will lead to an overall delay if they overrun their planned completion time**

● **know that a project is a planned enterprise to achieve a particular outcome**

● **know that a compound project is a project made up of a series of parts, activities or even smaller projects.**

Precedence Table

Creating a **precedence table** is the first part of managing a project.

All the necessary activities are listed along with length of time and whether they require other activities to be completed first.

For example, getting dressed and leaving home:

Activity	Immediate Predecessor	Duration (mins)
A: Put on underwear		1
B: Put on trousers	A	1
C: Put on shirt	A	1
D: Put on socks		1
E: Put on jumper	C	1
F: Put on coat	C	1
G: Put on hat	E	1
H: Put on shoes	A, D	2
I: Leave home	F, G, H	1

Activity Network

An **activity network** is a flowchart, read from left to right, that indicates the sequence of activities in a project.

The activity network for the getting dressed and leaving home example might look like this:

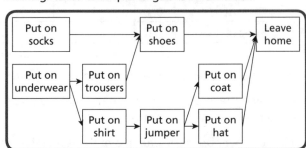

The way this network is constructed suggests that there are activities that can be done at the same time.

This is often the case if there are sufficient resources (i.e. people and money). For example, when decorating a house, one person could paint the living room whilst another paints the bedroom.

Activity-on-Node Network

An activity network for a project can be further refined to include timings.

The activities that need to be completed can be represented on a form of flowchart to indicate their duration and their dependence on completion of other activities.

The activities that take the longest are called **critical activities**.

This type of diagram is called an **activity-on-node network**. The activities are represented by points called **nodes** and the arrows between them are called **arcs**.

Here is an activity-on-node network for the getting dressed and leaving home example:

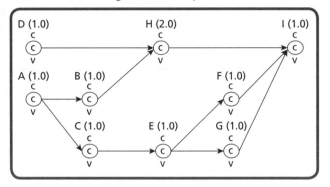

SUMMARY

- A precedence table is used to break a project down into separate activities.
- It shows the duration of each activity and the order of precedence, i.e. which activities need to be completed first.
- An activity network is a flowchart showing the sequence of activities.
- An activity-on-node network uses a node (a point on the network) to show each activity and its duration.
- The lines between nodes are called arcs.
- A critical activity is the activity that takes the longest time from start to finish, which would result in an overall delay if it overruns.

QUICK TEST

1. What does 'precedence' mean?
2. Define an activity network.
3. What are nodes?
4. What does the following notation represent on an activity-on-node diagram: A (1.0)?
5. What information is required for a precedence table?
6. List all the activities in order for wrapping a gift.

PRACTICE QUESTIONS

1. What would be the advantage of completing two activities at the same time? **[2 marks]**
2. If workers are ill, what might be the effect on a project? **[1 mark]**
3. Complete the table below to create a precedence table. **[4 marks]**

Activity	Immediate Predecessor	
A: Cook egg		
B: Make toast		
C: Butter toast		
D: Cook beans		
E: Put beans on toast		
F: Put egg on toast		
G: Serve		

Critical Activities

LEARNING OBJECTIVE

You need to be able to use early and late time algorithms to identify critical activities and to find the critical path(s).

The **critical path** is the path through a network, from start to finish, that takes the longest.

Delays in any of the activities along this path will result in an overall delay to the completion of the project, which could result in significant penalties or difficulties.

For example, if a contractor does not finish laying the tarmac on a road at the weekend (perhaps because they underestimated the quantity needed), there could be severe disruption to the traffic on Monday morning, which could have economic consequences.

It is, therefore, essential to identify the critical path and critical activities to reduce the risk of the project overrunning.

For the getting dressed and leaving home example, changing the duration of the activities slightly leads to the following precedence table:

Activity	Immediate Predecessor	Duration (mins)
A: Put on underwear		3
B: Put on trousers	A	1
C: Put on shirt	A	1
D: Put on socks		2
E: Put on jumper	C	1
F: Put on coat	C	2
G: Put on hat	E	1
H: Put on shoes	A, D	2
I: Leave home	F, G, H	1

This information can then be displayed on a more sophisticated activity network that uses nodes to give the following information.

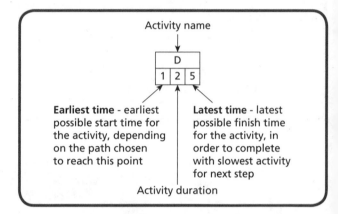

Using this new representation to complete the activity network for getting dressed and leaving home results in the network below:

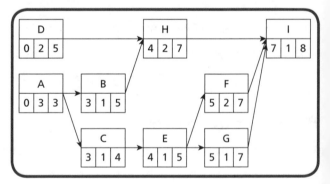

For example, for Activity H, the earliest possible 'arrival' time at this activity (start time) is when all the activities that precede it have been completed.

It is not possible to start putting on shoes until underwear (A), trousers (B) and socks (D) have been put on, i.e. after 3 minutes (underwear) + 1 minute (trousers) = 4 minutes.

Fill in all the earliest start times by sweeping forward through the entire network in this way.

The latest finish time for each activity can be found by working backwards through the network once the earliest start times and durations are known.

The latest time for the final activity is the start time plus duration. For I, the latest time = 7 + 1 = 8.

The preceding activities must have a finish time equal to the following activity minus its duration.

For example, activities H, F and G must all finish at 8 − 1 (from I) = 7.

Similarly, going backwards, the latest finish time for E must be the smallest number generated from F (7 − 2 = 5) or G (7 − 1 = 6), i.e. 5.

The critical path is the route through the network, from start to finish, that has no flexibility in the duration of the activities and will cause an overall delay if it overruns, i.e. for each of the activities in this path: latest time − earliest time = duration.

If there is any flexibility, this is called the **float** and is given by:

float = latest time − earliest time − duration.

For example, Activity D has a float of 5 − 0 − 2 = 3. This means it could start 3 minutes later and it, and all the activities after it, would still be completed in time for the first critical activity that follows after it (in this case Activity I).

The critical path for the getting dressed and leaving home example would therefore be:

A, C, E, F, I.

SUMMARY

- The critical path is the path through the network that will cause an overall delay if any of the activities on that path are delayed.

- The latest time for an activity is the latest time it can be completed without causing an overall delay to the project

- The earliest time for an activity is the earliest time that particular activity can start (when all preceding activities are completed).

- Float = the latest time – the earliest time – the duration, i.e. the extra time available to complete an activity.

QUICK TEST

1. Define the following:

    a) critical path

    b) latest time

    c) earliest time

    d) float

2. The duration of a particular activity is 2 days. It starts on day 4 and can finish by day 7. What is the float?

3. Explain why the activities in a critical path are critical.

4. How can the critical activities be identified from a completed activity network?

5. How can the latest finish times be calculated?

6. Activity Q leads to R and S. R has a latest finish time of 15 days and a duration of 2 days. S has a latest finish time of 17 days and a duration of 5 days. What is the latest finish time of Q?

PRACTICE QUESTIONS

1. The redevelopment of a block of flats is divided up into 8 activities:

Activity	Immediate Predecessor	Duration (weeks)
A		4
B	A	3
C	A	5
D	B, C	2
E	D	1
F	D	1
G	D	2
H	E, F, G	1

    a) Construct an activity network for this project.   **[7 marks]**

    b) List the critical path.   **[1 mark]**

    c) If the project starts on 1 March, when will it finish?   **[3 marks]**

2. Here is a precedence table for a project:

Activity	Immediate Predecessor	Duration (weeks)
A		2
B		1
C	B	1
D	C	1
E	C	2
F	A, D, E	1
G	F	1
H	F	2
I	G, H	1

    a) Construct an activity network for this project.   **[7 marks]**

    b) State why B is a critical activity.   **[1 mark]**

    c) The company is able to invest money to halve the completion time of any activity.

        Which activities should they choose?
        Justify your answer.   **[3 marks]**

    d) If the durations of all the activities identified in part c) are halved and the project
        starts on Monday 1 July, when should it finish?   **[3 marks]**

Gantt Charts

LEARNING OBJECTIVE

You need to be able to use Gantt charts (cascade diagrams) to present project activities.

A **Gantt chart** (cascade diagram) is a simple diagram that shows the durations and precedents of all the activities in a project with time along the x-axis. It provides a simple guide to running a project.

Typically, a Gantt chart starts with the first activity at the top left and runs through to the bottom right so that it looks like a cascade. (It can, however, be drawn starting from the bottom left and working up.)

Often, the critical activities are shown across the bottom.

A Gantt chart shows all activities, their start times, durations, end times and floats. Each activity will generally be on a separate line. It is easy, therefore, to see:
- any activities that can run concurrently
- the **timescale** of the entire project
- the critical path.

Gantt charts are useful for planning and scheduling projects. They help:
- assess how long a project should take
- determine the resources needed (for example, if two activities can be done at the same time, then individuals are needed to make that happen)
- plan the order in which to complete tasks
- manage the dependencies between tasks.

A: Put on underwear, B: Put on trousers, C: Put on shirt, D: Put on socks, E: Put on jumper, F: Put on coat, G: Put on hat, H: Put on shoes, I: Leave home

The solid vertical lines represent any dependencies, e.g. B and C need A to be completed first.

The dotted lines indicate a float, e.g. G takes only 2 minutes, can start at 5 minutes and only needs to be completed before I starts at 7 minutes.

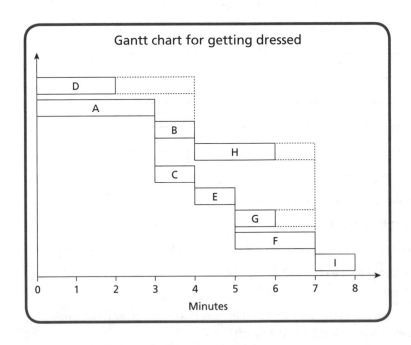
Gantt chart for getting dressed

In the exam, if you are asked to produce a Gantt chart, you will be given some graph paper and the solution should look like the graph below.

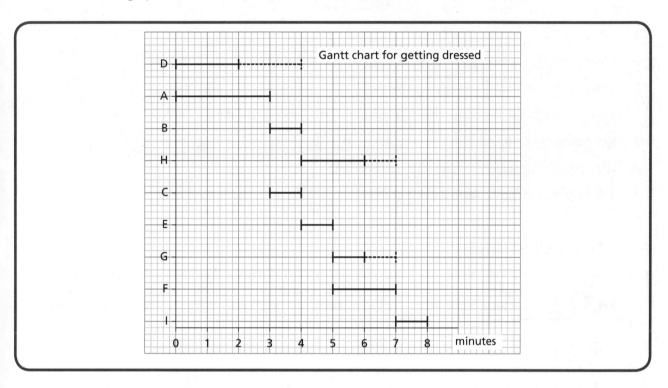

Gantt chart for getting dressed

The activities could have particular names and/or letters, which may or may not run in alphabetical order.

SUMMARY

- A Gantt chart shows the sequence and timing of events in a project.
- The x-axis indicates time.
- The float for an activity is shown by dotted lines.

DAY 5

QUICK TEST

1. What is a Gantt chart?

2. What is meant by 'timescale'?

3. What do the dotted lines on a Gantt chart indicate?

4. How are concurrent activities (ones that run at the same time) indicated?

5. What does the x-axis indicate?

6. How can you see the critical path on a Gantt chart?

7. What are the practical uses of a Gantt chart?

PRACTICE QUESTIONS

1. A construction project has the following activities and timings (G has the finish time missing):

Activity	Duration (days)	Earliest Start Time	Latest Finish Time
A	2	0	4
B	1	0	1
C	1	1	2
D	1	2	4
E	2	2	4
F	1	4	5
G	1	5	-
H	2	5	7
I	1	7	8

a) Draw a Gantt chart for the project assuming that the activities start as early as possible. **[4 marks]**

b) Assuming that I is dependent on completing G, what is the float for G (include this on your Gantt chart). **[3 marks]**

c) C and G both overrun by 2 days.

What is the earliest possible completion day now? **[2 marks]**

2. The refurbishment of a new factory has been split into several smaller projects
One of these projects has the following set of activities:

Activity	Immediate Predecessor	Duration (weeks)
A		4
B	A	3
C	A	5
D	B, C	2
E	D	1
F	D	1
G	D	2
H	E, F, G	1

a) Draw the Gantt chart of the project. [3 marks]

b) List the critical path. [1 mark]

c) Activities, B, D and F all overrun by 2 weeks.

Give the new expected completion date. [4 marks]

d) Following on from the situation in part c), after activity B is completed, the project manager decides to employ workers for 7 days a week instead of the 5 that they were originally working.

By how many weeks will the project now be delayed? [3 marks]

e) If each activity takes a week longer than planned and they start on 15 August, will project be completed in time for Christmas? [3 marks]

Probability

Probability is about trying to determine how likely it is that something will happen, i.e. the 'chance' or 'odds'.

This is essential for some business decisions, e.g. so that insurance companies can work out how much to charge their customers or local councils can plan how much salt is needed for gritting the roads in winter.

The Language of Probability

Experiment: A set of actions to find the result (outcome) of an activity, e.g. tossing a coin 100 times.

Event: A particular outcome, e.g. getting a head when tossing a coin.

Random event: An outcome that happens by chance, e.g. lottery numbers.

Experimental probability: The probability as determined by the results of an experiment. For example, if a piece of buttered toast is dropped 100 times and found to land butter-side down on 55 occasions, the experimental probability is 0.55

Theoretical probability: The number of ways of getting a particular outcome divided by the total number of possible outcomes. For example, if two dice are thrown and the numbers added, there are 6 ways of getting a total of 7 out of 36 possible outcomes, so the probability is $\frac{6}{36}$ or $\frac{1}{6}$.

This is shown in the **sample space** (table of outcomes) below.

+	1	2	3	4	5	6
1	2	3	4	5	6	7
2	3	4	5	6	7	8
3	4	5	6	7	8	9
4	5	6	7	8	9	10
5	6	7	8	9	10	11
6	7	8	9	10	11	12

Fair or unbiased: The outcomes are equally likely. For example, the chance of getting any number on a fair die is the same, i.e. $\frac{1}{6}$.

Exhaustive: All possible results are included. For example, if a bag contains blue, red and green balls, merely citing the probabilities of drawing a red ball or a green ball green would not be exhaustive. In this case, however, it would be possible to determine the probability of drawing a blue ball by subtracting the other possibilities from 1. If all outcomes are included, the sum must be equal to 1.

P(B): Probability of even B occurring, e.g. the probability of tossing a fair coin and getting a head, P(heads) = 0.5

Expected outcome: The probability of an outcome × the number of trials. For example, if the probability of winning a game is $\frac{1}{4}$ and the game is played 100 times, the expected number of wins would be $\frac{1}{4} \times 100 = 25$.

Complementary probability: the probability of the event not happening, i.e. 1 – the probability of the event.

Example

Alexa buys a bag of sweets and counts the contents. The sweets are red, yellow, blue, green or black and there is a total of 60 in the bag.
She calculates the experimental probabilities of getting the different colours as follows: red 0.27, blue 0.1, green 0.17 and black 0.25

How many yellow sweets did Alexa have?

The sum of the probabilities of all outcomes = 1, so the probability of yellow is:

P(yellow) = 1 – (P(red) + P(blue) + P(green) + P(black))
          = 1 – (0.27 + 0.1 + 0.17 + 0.25)
          = 1 – 0.79
          = 0.21

If the probability of getting a yellow is 0.21 and there are 60 sweets, the number of yellow must be:

0.21 × 60 = 12.6, i.e. 13 sweets
(The values that Alexa calculated must have been rounded to 2 decimal places. To give an exact result, she could have used fractions, e.g. $\frac{13}{60}$.

Example

After extensive trials, the probabilities for a particular dice were measured as:

Value	1	2	3	4	5	6
Probability	0.15	0.15	0.15		0.15	0.15

a) What is this probability of throwing a 4?

   P(4)   = 1 – (0.15 + 0.15 + 0.15 + 0.15 + 0.15)
          = 0.25

b) Can this dice be considered to be fair?

   No, because the probabilities are not equal after extensive trials.

c) Two pool players throw the dice to decide who breaks first. The highest value wins.

   If the first player throws a 3, what is the probability that the second player will break first?

   The probability of getting a 4, 5 or 6 and breaking first is:
   0.25 + 0.15 + 0.15 = 0.55

SUMMARY

- A sample space is a table showing all possible outcomes.
- The sum of the probabilities of all possible outcomes = 1.
- Expected outcome = probability × number of trials.
- Complementary probability is the probability of something not happening, i.e. 1 – the probability of it happening.

QUICK TEST

1. What is meant by 'expected outcome'?

2. a) In a fair pack of cards, what is the probability of getting a red queen?

   b) If all the hearts were removed from the pack, would the chance of getting a red queen increase or decrease?

3. In a boxing match, is it equally likely that either fighter will win?

4. With a fair coin, is the chance of getting a head 50%?

5. Gina thinks that the chance of a car being parked facing in a particular direction on one side of a two-way street is 50–50. Is she right?

6. If someone wanted to complete a survey of adults, would standing outside a football match give a random sample?

7. 65% of a population voted in an election. The Red Party won with 54% to 46%.
   What is the chance that a randomly selected person voted for the Red Party?

PRACTICE QUESTIONS

1. In a game, two dice are thrown and the scores added. The highest total score wins.
   Two children invent a rule whereby they have to nominate the number they are going to achieve before they throw.
   Henry chooses 5 and Gal chooses 8.

   Ignoring any draws (where both children roll their nominated numbers), how many times more often should Gal win? **[3 marks]**

2. The numbers on two spinners are added to give a total score.
   One spinner has even numbers from 2 to 8 and the other has odd numbers from 1 to 9.

   a) What are the chances of the total score being an even number? **[1 mark]**

   b) Which numbers are most likely to come up? **[2 marks]**

   c) If the first player gets a score of 7, what is the probability of the second player getting a score of more than double their score? **[4 marks]**

   d) Two players decide that if the total score is less than 10, one wins, and if it is more than 10, the other wins.

   Is this fair? Explain your answer. **[2 marks]**

3. In European roulette, there is a wheel with slots numbered 0–36.
   If the ball lands in slot 0, the casino wins.

   a) What is the probability that the casino will win on any single spin? **[1 mark]**

   b) In American roulette, there is an extra 00 where the casino also wins.

   What is the probability of the casino winning here? **[1 mark]**

   c) Which system is better for the casino? **[1 mark]**

4. A particular casino allows gamblers to choose three cards from a pack.
   If they get three of a kind (e.g. 3 nines), the casino will pay the gambler 100 times their bet.

   How does the casino make money? **[3 marks]**

Diagrammatic Representations

LEARNING OBJECTIVE

You need to be able to understand and apply Venn diagrams and simple tree diagrams.

Venn Diagrams

A **Venn diagram** is a way of visually representing the relationship between sets, groups or events using circles within a rectangle.

The outer rectangle encloses all possible values and is called the **universal set**.

Example

The following Venn diagram shows different groups as percentages of the population in a particular region of a country.

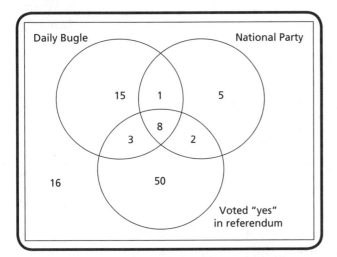

In this region, the total percentage of the population that:

- buys the *Daily Bugle* regularly is 15 + 1 + 8 + 3 = 27%
- voted for the National Party in the last election = 1 + 8 + 2 + 5 = 16%
- voted 'yes' in the referendum = 50 + 3 + 8 + 2 = 63%
- does not come in to any of the above groups = 16%

The reason why the percentages do not add up to 100% is that some sections have been counted twice or, in the case of the centre, three times.

The diagram illustrates the connection between these different groups (sets). For example, all the people who voted for the National Party and voted 'yes' in the referendum, are shown in the overlap or **intersection** of those two circles, i.e. 8 + 2 = 10%.

The percentage of people who did not vote 'yes' in the referendum is given by the total number outside that circle, i.e. 16 + 15 + 1 + 5 = 37%.

This could also have been calculated by considering the complementary probability, i.e. 100 − 63 = 37% (63% being the total who voted 'yes').

The Venn diagram can be used to determine probabilities. For example, the probability that a person chosen at random in this region buys the *Daily Bugle* regularly, voted National Party and voted 'yes' in the referendum would be 8% (the section where all three overlap).

It can also be used to calculate more complicated probabilities. For example, given that a person buys the *Daily Bugle* regularly, what is the probability that they voted 'yes' in the referendum?

The first part of the question indicates that the person is one of the 27% in the *Daily Bugle* circle.

The next step is to look at how many of those also fall into the 'voted 'yes'' circle, i.e. 8 + 3 = 11. The probability would then be $\frac{11}{27}$ = 0.407 (This is an example of conditional probability, which is explored further in the next section.)

Tree Diagrams

Tree diagrams are used to show the outcomes and probabilities in a sequence of events and are typically used to calculate the probability of a particular result.

They are called tree diagrams because the various possibilities branch out from left to right like a tree.

Example

To gain a particular qualification, students are required pass two maths papers.

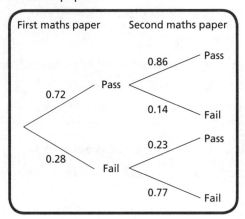

First maths paper   Second maths paper

- 0.72 → Pass
  - 0.86 → Pass
  - 0.14 → Fail
- 0.28 → Fail
  - 0.23 → Pass
  - 0.77 → Fail

The probability that a student will pass both papers is given by: $0.72 \times 0.86 = 0.619$

This is calculated by following the branches from left to right and multiplying the probability of passing the first paper by the probability of then passing the second paper.

To calculate the probability of getting at least one pass:

1. Identify the different routes that include at least one pass.
2. Multiply the probabilities along the branches for each of these routes.
3. Add the results.

Probability of pass–pass: $0.72 \times 0.86 = 0.619$
Probability of pass–fail: $0.72 \times 0.14 = 0.101$
Probability of fail–pass: $0.28 \times 0.23 = 0.064$
Probability of at least one pass: $0.619 + 0.101 + 0.064 = 0.784$

The same result could again be calculated using the complementary probability, i.e. by subtracting the probability of no passes (two fails) from 1:

Probability of at least one pass: $= 1 -$ probability of no passes (fail–fail)
$= 1 - (0.28 \times 0.77)$
$= 0.784$

SUMMARY

- The outer rectangle of a Venn diagram contains all possible occurrences (the universal set).
- A Venn diagram shows the relationship between different groups.
- Values in the areas where circles overlap (intersect) represent the numbers that fall into both or all of those groups.
- Multiplying the probabilities along the branches of a tree diagram, from left to right, gives the probability of that particular set of events happening.
- The sum of the probabilities of all the branches extending from a single point is equal to 1.
- Using complementary probability may involve fewer calculations than finding the probability of a result directly.

QUICK TEST

1. Group A contains 25 members and the intersection between Group A and Group B contains 8 members. If a person is in Group A, what is the probability that they are also in Group B?

2. In the Venn diagram example on page 88:

   a) what is the probability of choosing a person at random who does not buy the *Daily Bugle*, did not vote National Party and did not vote 'yes' in the referendum?

   b) if a person voted for the National Party at the election, how would they be expected to vote in the referendum? Explain your answer.

3. If the probability of succeeding in something is 0.17, what is the probability of **not** succeeding?

4. In the tree diagram example on page 89:

   a) what is the probability of passing the first maths paper?

   b) what is the probability of passing the second maths paper?

5. When tossing two fair coins:

   a) what is the probability of getting a head and a tail?

   b) what is the probability of not getting a head?

PRACTICE QUESTIONS

1. Look at the Venn diagram below:

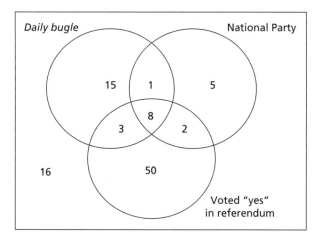

a) What is the probability of selecting a person at random who is a *Daily Bugle* reader, but did not voted for the National Party? **[2 marks]**

b) What percentage of the regional population voted 'yes' in the referendum and voted for the National Party, but do not buy the *Daily Bugle*? **[1 mark]**

c) What percentage of the regional population did not vote 'yes' in the referendum? **[2 marks]**

2. In a survey of 85 students, 42 got more than 60% in their Geography test, 37 got more than 60% in their History test and 12 got more 60% in both tests.

a) Construct a Venn diagram to show this information. **[4 marks]**

b) What is the probability that a student chosen at random got more than 60% in their Geography test, but not in their History test? **[1 mark]**

3. For a particular darts player, there is a 0.8 probability of hitting 20 with his first dart.
If he hits a 20, he has a 0.9 chance of hitting it again with his second dart.
If he misses, he has a 0.75 chance of hitting a 20 with the second dart.

Work out the probability of the darts player missing 20 with both darts. **[3 marks]**

4. When tossing three coins, what is the probability of two heads? **[3 marks]**

Combined Events

You need to be able to calculate the probability of combined events:

● both A and B

● neither A nor B

● either A or B (or both).

In the real world, there are some systems that will fail if one part of the system fails. For example, in a simplistic model, a helicopter will crash if the motor fails *or* if a rotor fails.

Similarly, a bicycle going downhill will be in trouble if both the front brake *and* the back brake fail.

If the front brake fails, the cyclist will have to apply the back brake much harder and the chance that it will fail increases. The probability of the back brake failing is **dependent** on the state of the front break.

However, whether the cyclist is wearing red or black will not affect the state of the back break. So, the probability of its failure is **independent** of shirt colour.

Example
To gain a particular qualification, students are required pass two maths papers.

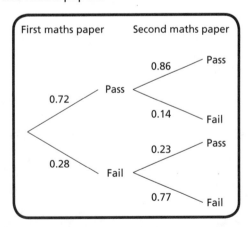

In this tree diagram, the probability of passing the second maths paper is dependent on the result of the first paper. A student has a much higher probability of passing the second paper if they passed the first.

What is the overall probability of passing the second paper?

Pass, Pass: $0.72 \times 0.86 = 0.6192$
Fail, Pass: $0.28 \times 0.23 = 0.0644$
Overall probability of passing the second paper =
$0.6192 + 0.0644 = 0.6836$

So, the probability of passing the first paper is
$P(P1) = 0.72$ and the probability of passing the second is $P(P2) = 0.6836$

If two events are independent, the probability of them both happening is found by multiplying the individual probabilities together:
$P(P1 \text{ and } P2) = P(P1) \times P(P2)$ (independent)

In this example:
$P(P1 \text{ and } P2) = 0.72 \times 0.86 = 0.6192$ (from the top line of the tree diagram)
But, $P(P1) \times P(P2) = 0.72 \times 0.6836 = 0.492$

These values are not equal – the events are not independent, they are dependent.
(This can be seen directly from the fact that the two branches leading to a 'Pass' in the second paper have different values.)

If the events are independent, the probability of the second event does not change when the first one occurs, i.e. the probability of B given that A has happened is same as the probability of B. Mathematically, this is written as:
$P(B \mid A) = P(B)$ (independent)

This all relates to conditional probability, where the second event depends on 'the condition' of the first event, i.e. which branch the process has gone down.

Example

In a particular town, the weather statistics were found to be as follows:

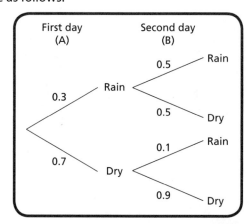

What is the probability that it rains on both days?

P(A and B) = 0.3 × 0.5 = 0.15

What is the probability that there is some rain over the weekend?

P(A or B) = 0.3 + (0.7 × 0.1) = 0.37

Another way is to consider all the possible outcomes involving rain over two days is:
P(R,R) = 0.3 × 0.5 = 0.15
P(R,D) = 0.3 × 0.5 = 0.15
P(D,R) = 0.7 × 0.1 = 0.07
Total = 0.37

What is the probability that there is no rain over the weekend?

P((A or B)′) = 1 – P(A or B) = P(A′ and B′)

An apostrophe indicates that the event does not happen, i.e. A′ means 'not A', so dry on the first day.

As indicated above, there are two ways of calculating this:
1 – P(A or B) = 1 – 0.37 = 0.63
P(A′ and B′) = 0.7 × 0.9 = 0.63

SUMMARY

- **Events are Independent if:**
  - ○ P(B | A) = P(B)
  - ○ P(P1 and P2) = P(P1) × P(P2)
- **Note that:**
  - ○ 'and' is also written as ∩ (intersection), i.e. P(A ∩ B)
  - ○ 'or' is also written as ∪ (union), i.e. P(A ∪ B).

QUICK TEST

1. What does independent mean?

2. If someone tosses five heads in a row with a fair coin, what is the probability that they will get a head on the next throw?

3. If the probability of an event happening is 0.27, what is the probability of it not happening?

4. In general, a particular athlete touches 1 in 20 of the hurdles she jumps. Given that she touches the second hurdle with a probability of 1 in 10 having touched the first, what can be said about these two events?

5. In the weather example on page 93, what is the probability of rain on Sunday if Saturday is wet?

6. The probability of Event A is 0.4 and the probability of Event B is 0.6. What is the probability of them both happening if they are independent?

7. What does 'A or B' look like on a Venn diagram, P(A ∩ B)?

8. What does 'A and B' look like on a Venn diagram, P(A ∪ B)?

PRACTICE QUESTIONS

1. A particular robot will cease to work if either of two components fails.
The probability of Component A failing on any given day is 1 in 1000.
The probability of Component B failing is 1 in 120.

What is the probability that the robot will work successfully for the day? **[4 marks]**

2. Samantha calculates the probability of seeing a particular bird on any given day in July as 0.28 and that of a different bird as 0.37
She also calculates that the probability of seeing them both is 0.15

What might Samantha conclude? **[2 marks]**

3. Erich has a bag of sweets. There are 11 blue, 5 red and 2 black.
His first three friends all take out a blue sweet by chance.
Erich bets his last friend that he will not choose a blue sweet.

Is this a wise bet? Explain your answer. **[2 marks]**

4. The probability of have a particular disease is 1 in 100 000.

A new test for the disease gives a positive result 98% of the time for people who have the disease and gives a negative result 95% of the time for those that do not have the disease.

If a randomly selected person tests positive, what is the probability that they actually have the disease? Comment on your results. **[6 marks]**

Expected Value

It is very important to be able to make judgements about the future in order to invest time or money. For example, is it worth buying insurance and how does the insurer calculate how much to charge clients?

This topic addresses the **expected value** of an investment loss or gain.

Example

A psychic claims to be able to predict the sex of a couple's next child.

They charge £30 and offer to return the money with an additional £10 'apology' if they are wrong.

Does the psychic make any money?

Given that the chance of having a boy or a girl is more or less equal, the psychic will be right 50% of the time and will keep the £30.

On the other occasions, again 50% of the time, they will give back the money and pay an additional £10 of their own money.

The total gain can be calculated as:
$$= (0.5 \times 30) + (0.5 \times -10)$$
$$= 15 - 5$$
$$= 10$$

The expected value (or mean value) of their gain each time they do this is £10. So, if they do this with 100 people, they should expect to make £1000.

In general, the probability of particular events is given by $p_1, p_2 \dots p_n$, where one of these events must happen and the total probability of all events is 1, i.e. $p_1 + p_2 + \dots p_n = 1$.

A value can then be assigned to each event, e.g. gain £30 or lose £10, and the expected value (like an average value) can be determined:

$$EV = p_1 v_1 + p_2 v_2 + \dots p_n v_n$$

Example

Olu decides to organise a game of chance to make money for charity at his school fête.

He plans to use two dice and add the two values when they are rolled.

He will give prizes of £2 for getting 9, £3 for 10, £4 for 11 and £5 for 12.

If he charges £1 a go, will he make any money?

The probability of getting:

- $9 = \dfrac{4}{36}$
- $10 = \dfrac{3}{36}$
- $11 = \dfrac{2}{36}$
- $12 = \dfrac{1}{36}$ (see sample space on page 84).

The value of each of these respectively (a loss or negative) is 2, 3, 4, 5, so:

Expected loss $= (\dfrac{4}{36} \times 2) + (\dfrac{3}{36} \times 3) + (\dfrac{2}{36} \times 4) + (\dfrac{1}{36} \times 5) = \dfrac{27}{36}$

Given that he charges £1 a go, he would expect to make £$1 - \dfrac{27}{36} = \dfrac{1}{4}$ pound or 25p per go.

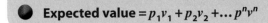

SUMMARY

- **Expected value** $= p_1 v_1 + p_2 v_2 + \dots p^n v^n$

1. In the example above, would Olu still make money if he returned the entry fee to winners?

2. What is meant by 'expected value'?

3. The psychic in the example on page 96 wants to run a promotion where they make an expected return of more than £5. What is the least they should charge if they still offer a £10 'apology'?

4. The cost of walking to work is 10p in shoe wear, whereas the bus costs £1.50. If Simon takes the bus 1 day in 10 (when it rains) and walks on all other occasions, calculate the expected travel costs incurred in a 220-day year.

5. Fred promised to pay his two children £1 each every time he is late to pick them up from their Saturday circus skills lessons. If he is late 1 in 8 times, how much might he expect to pay out over the year?

PRACTICE QUESTIONS

1. Every week Yahya takes part in an archery competition.
He keeps a record of his performance and notices that 1 in 3 times he makes it through to the final round and, if he is in the final round, he has a 20% chance of winning the £50 prize.

   If Yahya pays £5 to enter and does this for 30 weeks, how much does he stand to win or lose? **[6 marks]**

2. The probability of rain for a particular town is:

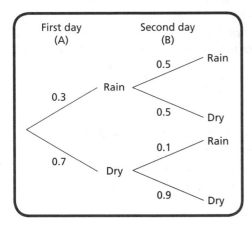

   If it rains on Friday, Anders bets his friend that it will rain on Saturday and Sunday too.

   How often can Anders expect to win this bet in one year? **[6 marks]**

3. Simone invents a new game for a charity event.
If a player throws less than 3 on a dice, she will give them double their money.
If they throw a six, they can throw again and subtract the new value from six.
Again they will win if the total is less than 3.

   Will Simone make money? Explain your answer. **[5 marks]**

Living with Uncertainty and Risk Analysis

LEARNING OBJECTIVES

You need to be able to:

● understand that many decisions have to be made when outcomes cannot be predicted with certainty

● use probabilities to calculate expected values of costs and benefits of decisions

● understand that calculating an expected value is an important part of such decision making.

Cost-benefit analysis is fundamentally a way of trying to predict the future and determine whether or not it is worth doing something.

For example, you might compare the 'cost' (in terms of effort and inconvenience) of having to carry an umbrella around all day, compared to the 'benefit' of staying dry if it rains.

The same kinds of choices are made when considering insurance, putting armour on a bomber plane or when a government decides whether to invest in either education for its citizens or building flood defences.

Cost benefit analysis helps determine whether or not something is worth doing – for example, the cost of having to carry an umbrella around all day compared to the benefit of remaining dry if it were to rain.

The calculation is made by comparing the **expected value** of the cost with the expected value of the benefit.

Example
Wynona has a plane to catch.
To get to the airport she will have to take a train.
If she misses the plane, she will have to pay for a new £200 ticket.
However, because she is on a budget, she does not really want to pay for an earlier, more expensive train ticket.

A comparison could work like this:

Earlier train:
Additional cost of having to buy early ticket = £25
Probability of missing plane and having to pay £200 = 0.05 (1 in 20 times there will be some delays and she will miss the plane even if she leaves early.)

Total = 25 + (0.05 × 200) = £35

Later train:
Additional cost of having to buy later ticket = £0
Probability of missing plane and having to pay £200 = 0.2 (1 in 5 times there will be some delays and she will miss the plane.)

Total = 0 + (0.2 × 200) = £40

This simple analysis suggests that she should leave earlier, but it also illustrates some of the difficulties in this process.

- It can be difficult to measure the probabilities in some situations, e.g. there are likely to be extensive statistics about trains and the delays at various times of the day, week or year.
- Giving a value to benefits or costs can also be difficult. What is the monetary value of the benefit of avoiding the stress of delays or the cost of missing half a day at the destination having got a later plane?
- Ethical or legal concerns are often ignored. To catch the earlier train, maybe Wynona had to leave her children to get up and go to school by themselves. Whilst more monetary value would be saved by protecting expensive houses from flooding, less people would be affected if the smaller, less valuable houses were protected.
- Generally calculations do not include the costs of the infrastructure, e.g. a logistics company does not pay for the roads it uses.

Generally the costs could include:

- initial costs, including perhaps research
- capital costs for equipment
- set-up costs
- overheads, salaries, etc.

Benefits might be:

- reduced costs
- increased revenue and/or efficiency.

Example

The cost of insuring an eReader worth £180 is £59 for 2 years (one-off payment) or £4 per month.

What probability of failure would make insurance worthwhile?

£59 for 2 years is about £30 a year, i.e. 6 years of insurance payments could buy a new eReader.

A probability of failure in any year of 1 in 6 would be needed to make it worthwhile, which seems unlikely.

The £4 per month insurance plan would take 45 months, about 4 years, to accumulate the value of a new eReader.

A probability of failure in any year of 1 in 4 is needed here, but it seems even more unlikely that 1 in 4 tablets will fail in a year or that a given tablet will fail in 4 years.

Given the progress of technology it might be that some families consider replacing eReaders with that regularity anyway.

As should be evident, insurance companies employ a lot of time and effort to make sure that their premiums make money for the company, which means they will pay out a lot less than they earn, i.e. customers will, on average, lose money.

Why, then, do people take out insurance? It might be that insurance is a legal necessity, such as car insurance, or that the loss might not be affordable, i.e. it might be better to pay a small amount each month than run the risk of having to pay out to replace or repair an expensive item in one go.

SUMMARY

- The benefit of a particular investment is the difference between the expected value of the outcome with and without it.

QUICK TEST

1. Work out the benefit of the following. Flood defences cost £200 million to build. They will last 20 years and reduce the annual risk of £1 billion pound damages from 1 in 10 to 1 in 100.

2. What is cost-benefit analysis?

3. How do insurance companies make money?

4. Estimate a reasonable insurance premium for a toaster. Is it worth taking out insurance on a low value item such as this?

5. A local council needs advice about flood defences. Should they invest in a scheme to protect against a 1 in 100 year event that would cause £5 billion pounds of damage or against a 1 in 10 year event that would cause £100 million worth of damage?

6. What are the risks and benefits associated with starting a new business?

7. What are some of the difficulties in evaluating costs and benefits?

8. List some of the costs and benefits associated with a project.

PRACTICE QUESTIONS

1. A £29.99 toaster has a 2% chance of breaking down and needing to be replaced in a five-year period.

   What cost of insurance would be worthwhile? **[4 marks]**

2. An insurance company offers two products.

   The first costs £250 and will pay the full cost of replacement.

   The second costs £150 and will pay only the amount above £500 (the voluntary excess).

   a) If the probability of a claim is 1 in 10 per year, which product is better value? **[3 marks]**

   b) At what probability of failure are both products equally good? **[2 marks]**

3. The probability of rain affecting groundwork on a building project is 0.3 and the cost of delays is £40 000.

   The company could rent a protective cover for £10 000.

   What should they do? **[2 marks]**

4. A game show involves two contestants randomly choosing from four envelopes that contain £1, £10, £100 and £1000.

   A contestant can elect to 'pay' £50 to go first.

   Is it worth doing this? Explain your answer. **[5 marks]**

5. A researcher has generated a formula to connect the probability of something going wrong with its cost.

   The probability of having a £90 repair is 1% and the probability of having a £10 repair is 9%, giving $R = 100 - 1000P$, where R is the cost of repair and P is the probability of that repair being necessary.

   What is the expected loss? **[4 marks]**

Control Measures

LEARNING OBJECTIVE

You need to be able to:

 understand that actions taken to reduce or prevent specific risks may have their own costs.

Having identified the **risks** associated with an investment or project, it is possible to evaluate any measures that could be taken to prevent or reduce these risks.

Any such measure will have a cost associated with it and this must be weighed up against the potential savings, i.e. each **control measure** is subjected to a **cost-benefit analysis** to determine its appropriateness.

Example

An IT project has a £24 000 penalty if the company does not deliver the software on time.

There are two key elements that might affect completion: the physics engine (P) and the rendering (R) packages.

The probability of the physics engine being delayed is 0.15 and the extra staffing costs to avoid delay are £5000.

Similarly for the rendering, there is a 0.25 chance of delay and £6000 spent on extra staffing would resolve that.

What is the expected loss if no extra personnel are employed?

Probability of P or R
$$= P(P) + P(R) - P(P) \times P(R)$$
$$\text{(assuming independence)}$$
$$= 0.15 + 0.25 - 0.15 \times 0.25$$
$$= 0.3625$$

Expected penalty
$$= 0.3625 \times 24\,000$$
$$= £8700$$

If extra staff are brought in for the physics engine only, the expected penalty (for the rendering being delayed) is:
$$= 0.25 \times 24\,000$$
$$= £6000$$

But there is an extra staff cost of £5000, so the total is:
$$= 6000 + 5000$$
$$= £11\,000$$

Similarly, controlling the rendering gives a total of:
$$= (0.15 \times 24\,000) + 6000$$
$$= £9600$$

The cost of doing both is 6000 + 5000 = £11 000

The preferable option here is to do nothing and hope for the best.

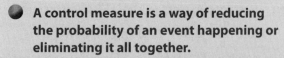

SUMMARY

- A control measure is a way of reducing the probability of an event happening or eliminating it all together.

- The cost of the event with the control measure includes the cost of the control measure, plus the expected costs with the new probabilities (which could be zero if the measure is completely effective at eliminating the risk).

QUICK TEST

1. What is a control measure?

2. What is the name of the process used to measure the effectiveness of a control measure?

3. Why might a company choose not to act upon the health and safety recommendations?

4. Why would a company employ control measures?

5. The probability of a £100 000 project going wrong is 15%. What would be the maximum cost of a worthwhile control measure?

6. It is possible to have a tracker in a car to monitor driving and help reduce the insurance costs. Suggest advantages and disadvantages.

PRACTICE QUESTIONS

1. **a)** A company employs 5100 people.

   The cost per day of someone being off work due to the flu is £300.

   The chance of this happening to an individual on any given day over the three-month winter period is 1 in 100.

   Estimate the expected cost to the company of employees being sick with the flu? **[4 marks]**

   b) There is a test that can identify which individuals will benefit from a flu vaccination.

   The test costs £10 per person and is 90% accurate.

   The vaccination costs £5 and gives 100% protection.

   Given that one-third of the employees will benefit from the vaccination, determine the benefit of the screening and vaccination programme. **[6 marks]**

2. A manufacturing company produces a product that has three main components.

   It has a contract to supply a major retailer, but will suffer a £1 million penalty if there are any delays.

   A delay will be incurred if any of the three parts are not ready on time.

   The probability of each part not being ready is as follows: Part A = 0.1, Part B = 0.2 and Part C = 0.3

   For Part A, it costs £10 000 for every 10% increased reduction in risk.

   For Part B, it costs £100 000 to half the risk of late delivery.

   For Part C, £25 000 reduces the risk of late delivery by 0.05

   The company has £100 000 to spend, how should it spend it? **[7 marks]**

3. An athlete is offered two banned substances.

   The first substance costs £5000 and will improve the athlete's chances of winning £100 000 from 50% to 60%. However, there is a 20% chance of a £20 000 fine.

   The second substance costs £3000 and will give the athlete a 7% better chance of winning. However, there is only a 10% chance of a £20 000 fine.

   What should the athlete do (assuming they can't take both)?

   Give all assumptions and arguments. **[5 marks]**

Graphs of Functions

LEARNING OBJECTIVE

You need to be able to sketch and plot curves defined by simple equations and know the shapes of linear, quadratic, cubic and exponential graphs.

Linear Graphs

Linear means line and this type of curve (the word used to describe the shape of a graph, even in this case) is completely straight.

A linear relationship can be represented in three different ways:

- as an **equation**, e.g. $y = 2x + 3$
- as a **table of values** (which can then be used to plot a graph)

x	y
0	3
1	5
2	7
3	9
4	11
5	13
6	15
7	17
8	19
9	21
10	23
11	25
12	27
13	29

- as a **graphical** (visual) representation.

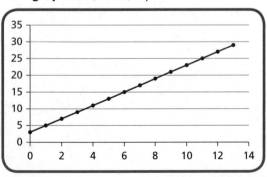

The equation for a straight line is generally written in the form:

$y = mx + c$

Where:

- m is the gradient (the change in y compared with the change in x)
- c is the y-intersect (the y-coordinate of where the line crosses the y-axis).

For the example above:

$m = \dfrac{4}{2} = 2$ (the x value increases by 2 between $x_1 = 6$ and $x_2 = 8$ and the y value increases by 4 from $y_1 = 15$ to $y_2 = 19$)

$c = 3$

Quadratic Graphs

In **quadratic** equations, the highest power of x is a square (x^2). They have the form:

$ax^2 + bx + c$

Quadratic equations produce parabolas when plotted, which are U-shaped if a is positive and upside-down if a is negative:

$y = 2x^2 + 2x - 4$

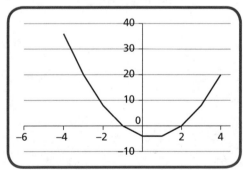

$y = -3x^2 - 9x - 6$

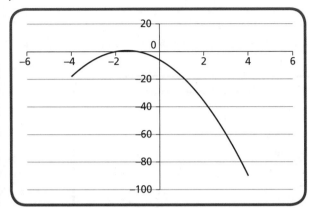

$y = -x^3 + 2x^2 - x - 2$

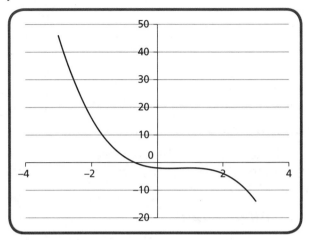

Cubic Graphs

In **cubic** equations, the highest power of x is a cube (x^3). They have the form:
$ax^3 + bx^2 + cx + d$

When plotted, if a is positive, cubic equations produce curves that start in the **third quadrant** (bottom left) and finish in the **first quadrant** (top right).

If a is negative, the curve is reversed – it starts in the **fourth quadrant** (bottom right) and ends in the **second quadrant** (top left).

$y = x^3 + 2x^2 - x - 2$

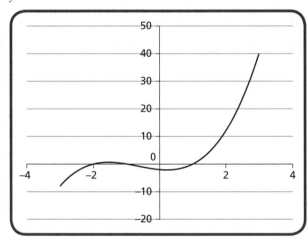

Exponential Graphs

Exponential curves have the variable as the **exponent** (power or index):
$y = ab^x$

They are generally obtained when the rate of change is proportional to the actual value, resulting in:

- **exponential growth** (where the exponent is positive, $y = ab^x$)
- **exponential decay** (where the exponent is negative, $y = ab^{-x}$).

For example, a cup of coffee will cool quicker when it is hotter, as there is a big difference between the coffee temperature and the surrounding temperature. As the coffee temperature approaches the surrounding temperature, there is less 'driving force' and the rate at which it cools decreases.

Exponential growth (i.e. population)

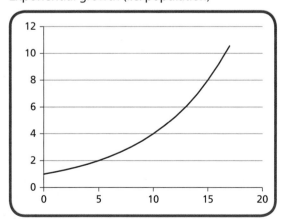

Exponential decay (i.e. cooling)

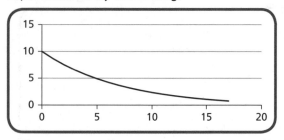

Both the above exponential curves become an **asymptote** – the line gets very close to the x-axis, but will never reach a zero value.

Sketching Graphs

There is an important difference between plotting a graph (e.g. from a table of values) and sketching.

Sketching involves giving the general shape of the curve and key points, such as the **intercepts** with the axes, **maximum** and **minimum points**, and **points of inflexion** (where the direction of the curve changes, e.g. in a cubic).

For example, $y = (x - 2)(x + 1)$ is a positive quadratic (U-shape) that crosses the x-axis at 2 and –1 and crosses the y-axis at –2 (it also has a minimum point at $x = 0.5$, but that is less obvious).

Scales

Scales should be carefully considered to ensure they are as clear as possible.

Also, when reading graphs, make sure that the scales start from zero when calculating relative factors. For example, in this graph, the value of video rentals in 1990 looks much higher than in 1995 because of the scale used.

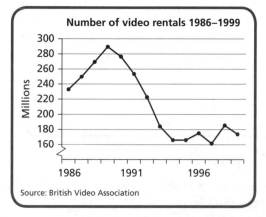

Source: British Video Association

1. Match each equation to the correct curve.

   A $y = 2x - 2$ **B** $y = x^2 + x - 2$ **C** $y = (x + 1)^2(x - 1)$

   D $y = \frac{1}{2}2^{-x}$ **E** $y = 2 \times 2^x$ **F** $y = (x - 2)(x - 1) \times (x + 1)(x + 2)$

   a)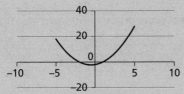

   b)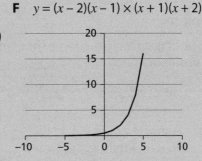

   c)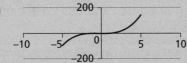

   d)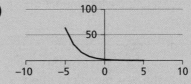

   e)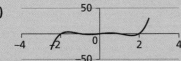

   f)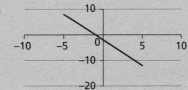

2. Plot the graphs of the following equations:

   a) $y = 3x + 2$ **b)** $3y + 4x = 12$ **c)** $y = x2 - 2x - 3$

PRACTICE QUESTIONS

1. A manufacturer works out that the amount of metal used to make a can is given by:

   $M = 6r^2 + \dfrac{600}{r}$

   where r is the radius of the cans in cm.

   Suggest the best radius to reduce costs.   **[5 marks]**

2. Two different energy companies have their prices as follows:
   Energy Less: 1.7p per unit
   Wind and Gas: 1.5p per unit + 1.1p fixed charge

   a) Illustrate the two price plans on the same graph.   **[4 marks]**

   b) Which company would be cheaper for 12 units?   **[1 mark]**

3. Shashi launces two rockets.
   The first follows a trajectory given by $y = 50x - x^2$
   The second follows a trajectory given by $y = 3x(30 - x)$.

   Which rocket travels:

   a) the highest and by how much?   **[4 marks]**

   b) the furthest and by how much?   **[1 mark]**

Intersection Points

Graphs can be used to compare values, e.g. to find out where one solution is better than or the same as another, or simply to determine when a quantity reaches a particular value.

For example, if an individual knows how much of any product they are likely to consume, it is possible to use this information to decide the best buying solution.

Example
Two different energy companies have their prices as follows:
Energy Less: 1.7p per unit
Wind and Gas: 1.5p per unit + 1.1p fixed charge

A graph shows that they give better value deals depending on consumption:

At what level of consumption of energy would it be preferable to switch suppliers?

The answer is given by the intersection (the point where the two lines meet).

Energy Less is less expensive below a consumption of 6 units (x-axis), but more expensive above that. If consumption is above 6 units, it would be preferable to switch to Wind and Gas.

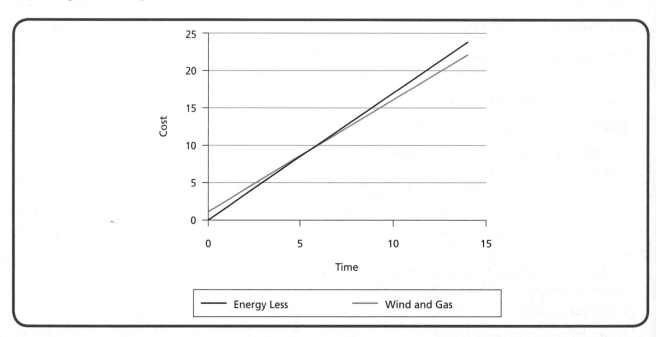

Extrapolation

Often mathematical models are developed to represent certain situations and to make calculations, and possibly predictions, about the other values.

However, there is a limit to the validity of these models. For example, they might work very well for a certain range of values, but results outside that range are less reliable.

Interpolation means finding values between known data points. **Extrapolation** means to find values beyond the range of the known data.

Example

Joe reads that with sensible eating and exercise he could healthily lose 1 kg of weight per week.

After the first two weeks he calculates that he is on track and will meet his target in another 10 weeks.

Why might this not be the case?

Weight loss will not always be linear. Whilst it might be a good model initially, it is probable that he will find it more difficult to lose weight as he gets thinner.

As an extreme example, if he did continue at the same rate, after two years he would have a negative weight!

SUMMARY

● **The following should be considered when reading and producing graphs:**
   ○ **What does the intersection of two lines mean?**
   ○ **Which side of the line is the important side? Does the value need to be bigger or smaller?**
   ○ **Is the range of values valid or are they too far outside the known data?**

QUICK TEST

1. A company decides to reduce the price of its products by £10 for every additional 100 units ordered. Is this sensible?

2. If a 10 mile journey costs £22 and a 15 mile journey costs £32, how much might it cost to travel 20 miles?

3. The voltage across a charging capacitor (electronic component) is given by: $9(1 - e^{-0.1t})$, where t is the time in hours. What is the maximum voltage?

4. If the growth is exponential, what can be said about the rate of change of y in relation to x as the x value increases?

5. The graphs of cost per unit of energy for two different companies intersect. What can be said about the points either side of this?

PRACTICE QUESTIONS

1. The table below shows average house prices in the north at the beginning of the century.

Use this data to predict what the average price is likely to be in 2020.
Comment on why this price might not be achieved. **[5 marks]**

Year / Quarter	Q1	Q2	Q3	Q4
2000	50 606	53 493	52 757	53 492
2001	54 720	53 951	59 752	59 510
2002	59 504	65 842	70 928	75 657
2003	81 226	87 082	93 334	98 448
2004	108 255	115 790	121 378	120 859

2. Sam wants to go swimming in the sea.
She knows that the current will be too strong if the tidal height is less than 4 m.

a) Between what times can she safely go swimming? **[2 marks]**

b) Sam thinks that it will always be safe to swim at these times. Is that true? **[2 marks]**

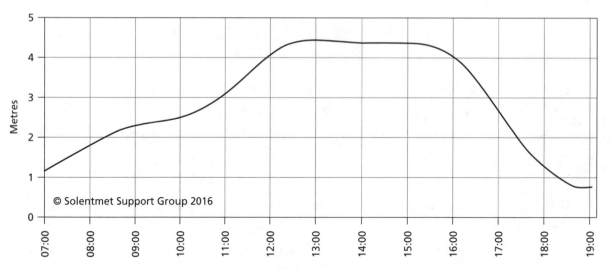

Tidal height

© Solentmet Support Group 2016

3. The drag of a car is given by $D = av^2 + b$, where a and b are constants and v is the velocity.
A table of values is obtained:

v	1	2	3	4	5
D	2.5	4.0	6.5	10.0	14.5

a) Estimate the values a and b. **[4 marks]**

b) Estimate the drag when $v = 0.5$ and when $v = 10$. **[3 marks]**

c) Which estimate is likely to be the most accurate and why? **[2 marks]**

4. Calvin wants to build a solar panel in his garden.
He knows the site will be in the shade if the sun is lower than an angle of 20° elevation.

For how much of the year will he not be able to generate electricity at midday if he points his panels due south? **[4 marks]**

Latitude: 60°N

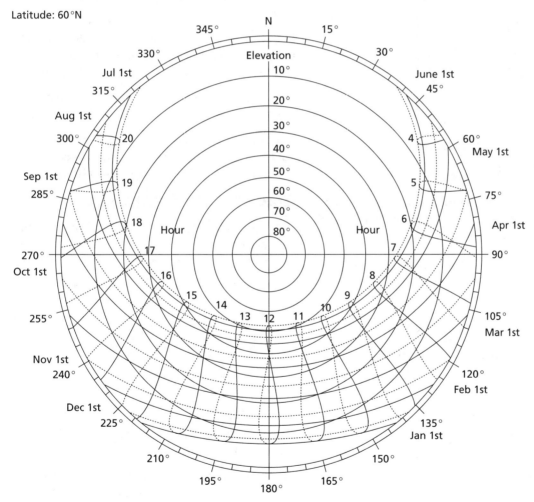

Computed using
Ecotech (ecotech.com)

Gradient

You need to be able to:

- interpret the gradient of a straight line as a rate of change
- interpret the gradient at a point on a curve as an instantaneous rate of change
- estimate rates of change for functions from their graphs.

Gradients and Rates of Change

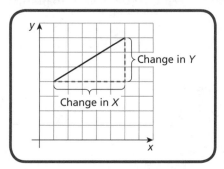

$$\text{Gradient} = \frac{changes\ in\ y}{changes\ in\ x} \text{ or } \frac{y_2 - y_1}{x_2 - x_1}$$

The gradient is a measure of how much one variable changes in relation to a change in another. In this case, the **rate of change** of y in relation to x.

For a straight line, the gradient or rate of change will be the same at any point on the line.

Example
A phone company installs an internet terminal at an airport.
It charges a £1 connection fee and £2 an hour.
A graph might look like this:

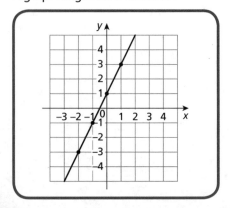

This general equation for a straight line graph is:
$y = mx + c$, where m is the gradient and c is the **y-intercept**.

In this case, the cost per hour is the rate of change or gradient (m) and the connection fee is the fixed cost or y-intercept (c).

This gives, $P = 2t + 1$, where t is the time in hours and P is the price.

Whilst the straight line could continue for negative values of x, this would correspond to negative values of t and would make no sense in this situation.

Gradients at a Point on a Curve

The gradient at a point on a curve is the gradient of the **tangent** line.

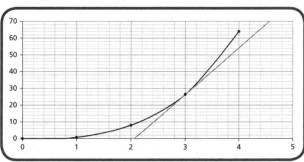

The gradient can then be found by considering two points that the tangent line goes through.

Choose points with coordinates that are easy to read. For example, to find the gradient at $x = 3$, draw the tangent line and choose values that are easy to read, i.e. (2.2, 4) and (4.2, 60):

$$\frac{(60 - 4)}{(4.2 - 2.2)} = 28$$

Maximum and Minimum Points

At local **maximum** or **minimum points** the gradient is zero. The reverse is often used to find these key points.

For example, on page 107 there is an exam question on finding the optimum radius for a can. This can be done by finding the point where the gradient is equal to zero ($m = 0$).

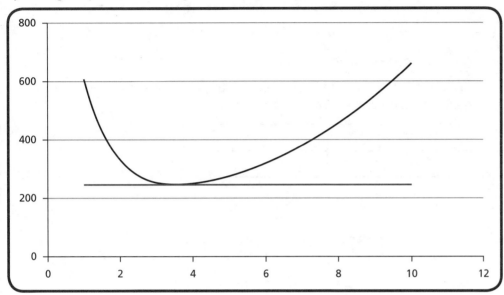

In this case, the point where $m = 0$ (minimum point) occurs when the x value (which represents the radius of the can) is 4 cm.

SUMMARY

- **The equation for a straight line is $y = mx + c$, where m is the gradient and c is the y-intercept.**
- **The gradient of a line is the rate of change of the y value in relation to the x value.**
- **The gradient of the tangent to a curve is the instantaneous rate of change at that point.**
- **The maximum or minimum values occur at the point where the graph has a gradient of zero.**

QUICK TEST

1. What is an instantaneous rate of change?

2. The cost of a taxi fare is calculated by adding a charge of £1 a mile to a fixed fee of £2.50.

   a) What is the rate of change of cost in relation to distance?

   b) What is the equation connecting the variables?

3. If the gradient at a particular point can be estimated by considering the line between the two points either side, estimate the gradient at $x = 1$ and $x = 2$ for the following curve.

x	0	0.5	1	1.5	2	2.5
y	0	0.25	1	2.25	4	6.25

4. If a value increases by 5% a year, what will happen to the rate of change of that value in relation to time as time passes?

5. The rate at which water drains from a tank depends on the height of water in the tank. What can be said about the time taken to fill a bucket from this tank when it is nearly full and when it is nearly empty?

6. What is the general equation of a straight line and what do the letters represent?

7. Phone Company A has a higher rate of change of cost in relation to time than phone Company B, but B has a higher fixed cost. Which is likely to offer better value with time?

PRACTICE QUESTIONS

1. The fuel consumption of a particular vehicle is given by:

$F = 0.01v^3 + 2v$, where F is the fuel consumption in cc/s and v is speed in m/s.

Estimate the point at which the rate change of fuel consumption in relation to speed exceeds 14 cc/m.   **[4 marks]**

2. Lewis measured the growth of his bamboo plant every night and recorded the results:

Day	1	2	3	4	5	6	7
Height (cm)	5	9	13	18	20	23	27

   a) Which day showed the greatest rate of growth?   **[1 mark]**

   b) Which day had the slowest growth?   **[1 mark]**

   c) If the plant had grown at the fastest rate until day 7, how tall would it have been?   **[3 marks]**

   d) What might cause the variation in growth?   **[1 mark]**

3. The graph shows the state of the tide at the entrance to Chichester Harbour.

   a) When was low tide?   **[1 mark]**

   b) How fast was the tide coming in at 1 pm?   **[1 mark]**

   c) Estimate the maximum rate of change of height.   **[2 marks]**

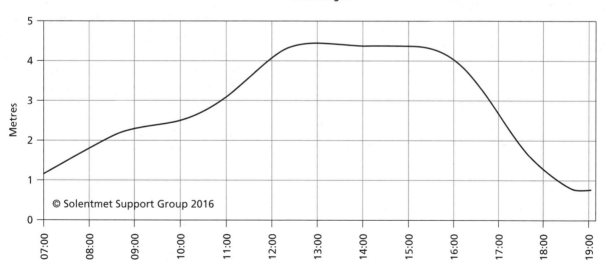

Tidal height

© Solentmet Support Group 2016

Average Speed

LEARNING OBJECTIVE

You need to know that the average speed of an object is given by $\frac{\text{distance travelled}}{\text{time taken}}$.

The **average speed** of an object is given by the distance it travels divided by the time taken to travel that distance (hence the units: miles per hour or metres per second):

$$\text{speed} = \frac{\text{distance travelled}}{\text{time taken}}$$

$$v = \frac{s}{t}$$

where:

- v is speed
- s is distance
- t is time.

For example, if a car travels 240 miles in 4 hours, it is travelling with an average speed of $\frac{240}{4} = 60$ mph.

Example

A driver travels at 30 mph for 30 mins and then at 70 mph for the next 1 hour.

What is her average speed?

This is a slightly trickier question because the distances are not given.

The distance, s, travelled in the first part is:

$$v = \frac{s}{t}$$

$$s = vt$$

$$s = 30 \times 0.5 = 15 \text{ miles (30 minutes = 0.5 hours)}$$

For the second part:
$$s = 70 \times 1 = 70 \text{ miles}$$

The speed is the total distance divided by the total time:

$$v = \frac{(70 + 15)}{(1 + 0.5)} = 56.7 \text{ mph}$$

SUMMARY

- The average speed is $\frac{\text{distance travelled}}{\text{time taken}}$
- $v = \frac{s}{t}$
- $s = vt$
- $t = \frac{s}{v}$

QUICK TEST

1. How long does it take to drive 100 miles at 70 mph?

2. Why is the speed given by $\frac{\text{distance travelled}}{\text{time taken}}$ only an 'average' speed?

3. A traffic speed camera takes two photos of a car. The photos show how far the car travels in half a second by comparing the change in position to white lines on the road. The distance between white lines is the equivalent of 5 mph.

   a) How many white lines would be covered if the motorist is travelling at 70 mph?

   b) What is the distance between the white lines? (Use 1 mile = 1610 m)

4. If the distance to a city is 65 miles, how much time would be saved by driving on the motorway (speed limit 70 mph) compared to the local A road (speed limit 50 mph)?

PRACTICE QUESTIONS

1. Erich has to drive from Inverness to Aviemore to drop off his mother.
   He will then continue to Aberdeen for some shopping before returning back to Inverness.
   He thinks he can drive the first part at about 30 mph, the second part around 50 mph and the return to Inverness at 70 mph.

   a) If Erich leaves at 9 am and needs to be home by 6 pm, how long can he spend in Aberdeen?   [6 marks]

   b) What is his average speed for the round trip?   [2 marks]

Distance Chart (in Miles)

Aberdeen								
63	Aviemore							
192	192	Berwick on Tweed						
179	175	146	Ayr					
216	223	92	94	Carlisle				
129	124	64	79	92	Edinburgh			
157	60	196	141	211	131	Fort William		
146	138	110	33	95	43	116	Glasgow	
105	28	220	207	260	154	64	175	Inverness

Speed and Acceleration

LEARNING OBJECTIVE

You need to know that the gradient of a distance–time graph represents speed and the gradient of a velocity–time graph represents acceleration.

The previous section showed that the speed of an object is given by distance divided by time, more precisely, the rate of change of distance with time.

Therefore, for a **distance–time graph**, the gradient is the speed.

The rate of change of speed with time is the definition of **acceleration**. Therefore, the gradient of a **speed–time graph** (or velocity–time graph) is the acceleration.

The **average acceleration** is the change in speed divided by the time taken for this change.

For example, if a car is travelling at 10 m/s and accelerates to 20 m/s in 5 seconds, its average acceleration would be $\frac{(20 - 10)}{5} = 2$ m/s^2.

Example

The position of a piston in an engine is given by the following graph:

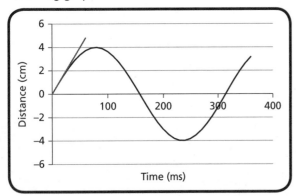

From graphical estimates, produce a graph of speed against time and acceleration against time.

The maximum rate of change (speed) is when the time is zero (and again at about 314 ms).

When the distance is at a maximum, the speed is zero (gradient is zero).

Getting the gradient could be a little difficult, but the red line shows a gradient of around 0.08 cm/ms or about 0.8 m/s.

Continuing this for other key points and plotting them gives:

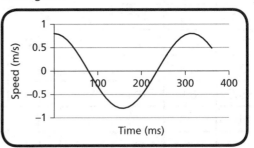

Again, identifying the times where the speed is at a maximum or minimum and where the gradients are a positive and negative maximum leads to the following graph for acceleration:

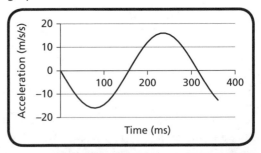

SUMMARY

● **Average acceleration is the change in speed divided by the time taken for the change.**

● **The gradient of a distance–time graph is speed.**

● **The gradient of a speed–time graph is acceleration.**

1. What does the gradient of a speed–time graph represent?

2. What is the rate of change of distance with time?

3. The distance–time graph for the movement of an object is a straight line. What can be said about the acceleration?

4. Car A goes from 0–60 mph in 5.4 seconds. Car B goes from 0–50 mph in 4.9 seconds. Which car has a higher acceleration?

PRACTICE QUESTIONS

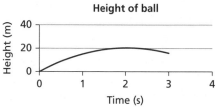

Height of ball

1. The graph on the right shows the position of a ball being thrown. Estimate the acceleration. **[5 marks]**

2. On the right is a speed–time graph for two athletes competing in the same race:

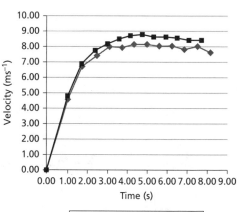

a) Which athlete wins? Explain your answer. **[2 marks]**

b) What is the maximum acceleration? **[2 marks]**

c) Estimate the acceleration at around 3 seconds for Athlete B. **[1 mark]**

d) What happens to Athlete B after about 5 seconds? **[1 mark]**

3. Describe what happens in the motion of the object below. **[8 marks]**

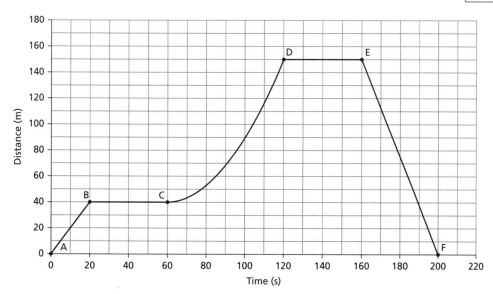

The Functions a^x and e^x

In an **exponential function** the variable (argument) is the power of a constant, e.g. a^x.

Many events in the real world are exponential. In February 2015, the exponential rise of the mobile phone, and particularly that of smartphones, was detailed.

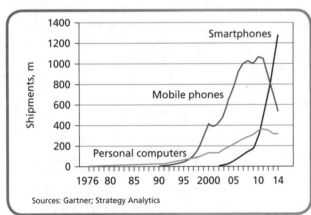

Sources: Gartner; Strategy Analytics

Exponential growth is also shown by computer memory (Moore's Law), population growth, diseases and compound investment.

It is important to understand the basics of such growth, i.e. the mathematics behind it and the calculations used, to help solve problems, such as 'when will there be more smartphones than people?'

The Function a^x

You need to be able to use the button (or equivalent) on a calculator to work out values of the function a^x:

a) $2^5 (= 32)$ **b)** $5^0 (= 1)$ **c)** $3^{-2} (= \frac{1}{9}$ or $0.11111i)$
d) $1^{-7} (= 1)$

Check that you get the answers shown in brackets on your calculator before continuing.

A table of values and graph is given for two exponential functions below.

x	$y = 2^x$	$y = 3^x$
−4	0.0625	0.012345679
−3	0.125	0.037037037
−2	0.25	0.111111111
−1	0.5	0.333333333
0	1	1
1	2	3
2	4	9
3	8	27
4	16	81

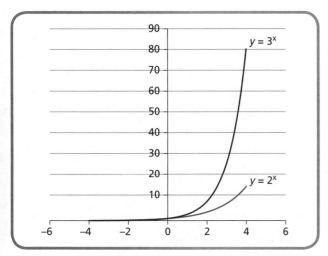

As can be seen, both graphs have a similar shape to the smartphone graph. All exponentials have this shape and all pass through 1 on the y-axis (as anything to the power of zero is 1).

If the power is positive, the curve will rise up from left to right and will have a **positive argument.**

If the power is negative, the curve will descend from left to right and have a **negative argument**.

Equations of the Form $a^x = b$ and $e^{kx} = b$

Just as the **inverse** of multiplication ($\times$) is division ($\div$), the inverse for exponentials ($a^x = b$) is logarithms ($x = log_a b$).

$2^3 = 8 \rightarrow log_2 8 = 3$

Here the base is 2 and the power is 3.

In **base 10**, for $2^x = 8$, $x = \dfrac{log 8}{log 2} = 3$

With the decimal system, all numbers are already in base 10, and the calculator log button is also in base 10. Base 10 is used in solving the following.

Example

a) $7^x = 24$

$x = \dfrac{log 24}{log 7} = 1.633196595$

b) $7^x = 5$

$x = \dfrac{log 5}{log 7} = 0.8270874753$

The **ln** button on a calculator is for natural logarithms and is in base e.

For $e^x = 8 \rightarrow x = ln 8$

Here the base is e and the power is x.

Note, $ln(e) = 1$ as they are the inverse of each other.

Generally, if $e^{kx} = b \rightarrow x = \dfrac{ln b}{k}$

The Number e – The Base of Natural Choice

Just as π has a special place in mathematics, so does the number e (2.718281828…).

Like π, e is irrational and occurs frequently in the real world. Therefore, it has many uses and can help solve many real life problems.

Example

If £1 is invested for one year at 100% interest rate, how much would it be worth at the end of the year?

The immediate simple interest answer is £2, but this does not take account of any compounding.

£1 @ 100% pa	In 1 year =	$1 \times (1 + \dfrac{1}{n})^n$
Compounded	n	**After 1 year**
Yearly	1	2
Monthly	12	2.61303529
Daily	365	2.714567482
Hour	8760	2.718126692
Every second	31 536 000	2.718281781

As the table shows, the greater the degree of compounding the closer the answers is to e. Mathematicians were able to confirm this as n tends towards infinity.

This and other examples show why e is the natural language of growth.

Example

a) If $e^x = 8$, what is the value of x?

$x = \dfrac{ln 8}{ln(e)} = \dfrac{ln 8}{1} = ln 8 = 2.079441542$

b) If $e^{2x} = 8$, what is the value of x?

$x = \dfrac{ln 8}{2} = 1.039720771$

Plotting $y = e^x$ Curves

The graph of $y = e^x$ has the same features as other exponentials, plus additional features that make it unique.

The gradient at any point on the graph of $y = e^x$ is the same as the y value of that point. For example, if $x = 2$ then $y = e^2 = 7.38905\ldots$ and the gradient at that point is also $7.38905\ldots$

x	$y = e^x$	$y = e^{2x}$	$y = e^{-0.5x}$
−4	0.018315639	0.000335463	7.389056099
−3	0.049787068	0.002478752	4.48168907
−2	0.135335283	0.018315639	2.718281828
−1	0.367879441	0.135335283	1.648721271
0	1	1	1
1	2.718281828	7.389056099	0.60653066
2	7.389056099	54.59815003	0.367879441
3	20.08553692	403.4287935	0.22313016
4	54.59815003	2980.957987	0.135335283
5	148.4131591	22026.46579	0.082084999
6	403.4287935	162754.7914	0.049787068

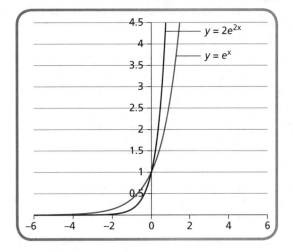

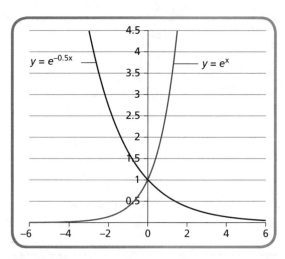

When sketching such curves, remember the basic shape, argument and the shared (0, 1) point. You also need to consider what happens to values of y if x is small or large.

Example

Rabbits were introduced onto an island.

t years after they were introduced, the number of rabbits, P, is modelled by the equation:

$$P = 120e^{\frac{1}{7}t}$$

where t is a real number and greater than zero.

a) Write down the number of rabbits that were introduced to the island.

At the start $t = 0$, so $P = 120e^0 = 120$

b) In which year after introduction will the number of rabbits exceed 700?

$$120e^{\frac{1}{7}t} = 700$$
$$e^{\frac{1}{7}t} = \frac{700}{120} = \frac{35}{6}$$
$$\frac{1}{7}t = \ln\frac{35}{6}$$
$$t = 7\ln\frac{35}{6} = 12.24512 \text{ years}$$

The number of rabbits will exceed 700 in the 13th year.

Example

A radioactive substance decays at rate of 13% per hour. Confirm that after 5 hours, less than half the radioactive substance would be left.

Amount after n hours $= 0.87^n$

If $n = 5$, $0.87^5 = 0.49842\ldots$

This is less than 0.5 (half).

Example

The spread of a disease is recorded.
The number of cases in months 5, 6 and 7 is as follows:

Month (t)	5	6	7
Number of cases (n)	335	1073	3435

This can be modelled by the equation $n = 3.2^t$

a) How many cases where there after 3 months?

$t = 3$, so $n = 3.2^3 = 32.768$

So, 32 cases

b) What is the value of t when there are 10 000 cases?

$3.2t = 10000$

$t = \dfrac{\log 10000}{\log 3.2} = 7.91844$ hours

$= 7$ hours 55 minutes 6 seconds

c) What was the value of t when the disease was first discovered?

$t = 0$

SUMMARY

- Exponentials occur naturally in the real world in many different ways.

- Graphs of exponentials have a similar shape and argument.

- They all go through (0,1) as anything to the power of 0 is 1.

- The power button on a calculator can be used to find a^x.

- For most numbers, base 10 can be used with the log button, e.g. if $a^x = b$, $x = \dfrac{\log b}{\log a}$

- e is used as the standard base for exponential functions.

- For base e, use the ln button, e.g. if $e^{kx} = b$, $x = \dfrac{\ln b}{k}$

- The gradient at any point on the graph of $y = ex$ is equal to the y value at that point.

- Knowledge of exponentials can help solve many real-life problems.

QUICK TEST

1. What is an exponential function?

2. Sketch the graph of an exponential function with a positive argument.

3. Sketch the graph of an exponential function with a negative argument.

4. Calculate the value of:

    a) $3.7^{2.1}$

    b) $2.5^{0.4}$

    c) $-4^{0.52}$

    d) $2.9^{-3.5}$

    e) $16^{-0.5}$

5. Calculate the value of:

    a) $e^{2.1}$

    b) $e^{0.4}$

    c) $-e^{0.52}$

    d) $e^{-3.5}$

    e) $e^{-0.5}$

6. Solve the following

    a) $2^{x} = 32$

    b) $8^{x} = 32$

    c) $5.2^{x} = 12.5$

    d) $8.7^{x} = 0.72$

7. If $N = 3.5^{0.7t}$, where N is the size of the population of bacteria and t is the time in hours, how long will it take for the population to double?

8. The amount of money in a savings account is given by $M = e^{t}$, where M is the multiplying factor applied to the initial amount of money and t is the number of decades. What is the rate of growth of the savings after 10 years?

PRACTICE QUESTIONS

1. The amount of yeast in a colony can be modelled by the following equation:

   $A = 2500\, e^{0.042t}$, where t is the time in hours.

   a) What is the initial size of the colony?   **[1 mark]**

   b) Sketch the graph for the first 5 hours.   **[2 marks]**

   c) How big is the colony after 3 hours?   **[1 mark]**

   d) How long will it take the colony to double in size?   **[3 marks]**

   e) Alysha says, 'As time goes on, the time it takes for the colony to double in size will lessen.'

      Is she right? Justify your answer.   **[3 marks]**

2. Manu likes to drink his tea when it is 35°C.

   He measures the temperature with time and gets the following results:

Time (min)	0	10	20	30	40
Temp (°C)	100	70	50	40	30

   Manu thinks that the temperature can be modeled by $T = 20 + 80e^{-0.05t}$, where T is the temperature in degrees Celsius and t is the time in minutes.

   a) Confirm that the equation is correct (allowing for experimental error).   **[2 marks]**

   b) What will the final temperature be and why?   **[2 marks]**

   c) Sketch the graph produced.   **[2 marks]**

   d) When is the tea cooling most quickly and what is the rate of change of temperature at this point?   **[3 marks]**

Exponential Growth and Decay

There are many examples of growth and decay in real life from natural sciences (e.g. diseases, population, radiation, half-life and cooling) to social sciences (e.g. GDP per capita, compound interest, depreciation and urbanisation) and there is a need to be able to formulate and use exponential functions to model such cases.

Growth and Decay Functions of the Form $y = Ca^x$ and $y = Ce^{kx}$

When considering whether an event is growing or decaying, there needs to be a starting point (the origin) in time.

Time is normally represented on the x-axis, so in the table below it is assumed that x starts at zero and increases as time goes by, or $x \geq 0$.

Form	Value of Constant	Growth or Decay
$y = a^x$	a > 1	growth
$y = a^x$	0 < a < 1	decay
$y = a^{-x}$	a > 1	decay
$y = e^{kx}$	k > 0	growth
$y = e^{kx}$	k < 0	decay

Example
A new car depreciates by 20% every year.

Write a formula for its value (V) after x years.

V is going down, so it is a decay formula.

Reducing by 20% is the same as multiplying by 0.8 – this is the a value.

So, $V = 0.8^x$ and $0 < a < 1$.

Example
The population (P) of a town is increasing at 5% every year.

Write a formula for P after x years.

$a = 1.05$ (100% + 5%) and $a > 1$

So, $P = 1.05^x$

Remember: $\dfrac{1}{1000} = \dfrac{1}{10^3} = 0.001$

Rules of indices: $(a^m)^n = a^{mn}$

Example
Atmospheric pressure (P) decreases by 12% every 1000 m.

At sea level, the pressure is 1013 hPa (assuming normal weather conditions).

What is the formula that gives the pressure (P) in terms of the height (h)?

$a = 0.88$ (100% – 12%) and at $h = 0$ (sea level), $P = 1013$ hPa

Time is also replaced by height (h) and the decrease is for every 1000 m, so:

$P = 1013 \times (\dfrac{0.88}{1000})^h = 1013 \times (0.88 \times 10^{-3})^h$

Using Exponential Functions to Model Growth and Decay

As with most problems in the real world, there are many routes to the same solution. Two preferred methods are shown here for a variety of examples.

Example 1
The value of a house is £150 000 when first purchased and increases by 8% per year.

How many years will it take to have doubled in value form its original price?

Let V = value, n = number of years required, original price is £150 000 and the desired price is £300 000.

So, $300\,000 = 150\,000 \times (1.08)^n$ and n needs to be found.

Method 1

$$\frac{300\,000}{150\,000} = (1.08)^n$$

$$2 = (1.08)^n$$

$$\frac{\log 2}{\log 1.08} = n$$

$$n = 9.006$$

Method 2 (Using Log Rules)

$$\frac{\log 300\,000 - \log 150\,000}{\log 1.08} = n$$

$$n = 9.006$$

It will take around 9 years for the property to double in value.

Example 2

A process can be modelled by the equation $y = Ce^{kx}$.

If $y = 30$, $C = 10$ and $k = 0.15$, find x.

The equation is $30 = 10e^{0.15x}$ and can be solved as follows:

Method 1

$$\frac{30}{10} = e^{0.15x}$$

$$3 = e^{0.15x}$$

$$ln3 = 0.15x$$

$$x = \frac{ln3}{0.15} = 7.324081924$$

Method 2 (Using Log Rules)

$$x = \frac{ln30 - ln10}{0.15}$$

$$x = \frac{3.401197382.. - 2.302585093...}{0.15}$$

$$x = 7.324081924$$

Example 3

The following equation can be used to model the temperature of a large container of water t hours after it has boiled and the heating has been turned off:

$$\theta = 22 + 78e^{kt}$$

where θ is the temperature in Celsius at time, t.

a) What is the initial temperature at $t = 0$ and does the answer makes sense?

At $t = 0$, $\theta = 22 + 78e^{k(0)} = 22 + 78e^0 = 100°C$

As this is the boiling temperature of water (at ground level), this seems to make sense.

b) Thirty minutes later the water had a temperature of $65°C$.

Show that $k = 1.19$ (3 sf)

$t = 0.5$ hours (remember, t is expressed in hours)

Method 1

$$65° = 22 + 78e^{0.5k}$$

$$65 - 22 = 78e^{0.5k}$$

$$\frac{43}{78} = e^{0.5k}$$

$$ln\,\frac{43}{78} = 0.5k$$

$$k = \frac{ln\frac{43}{78}}{0.5} = 1.191017$$

Method 2 (Using Log Rules)

$$65° = 22 + 78e^{0.5k}$$

$$65 - 22 = 78e^{0.5k}$$

$$ln43 - ln78 = 0.5k$$

$$k = \frac{ln43 - ln78}{0.5}$$

$$k = 1.191017$$

c) How many minutes does it take for the temperature to reach $30°C$?

Here $C = 30$ and $k = 1.191017$ (from part **b)**)

$30 = 22 + 78e^{1.191017\,(t)}$ and t needs to be found

$$30 = 22 + 78e^{1.191017(t)}$$

$$8 = 78e^{1.191017(t)}$$

$$ln\,\frac{8}{78} = 1.191017(t)$$

$$t = \frac{ln\frac{8}{78}}{1.191017} = 1.912035242 \text{ hours}$$

$t = 1$ hour 54 minutes 43 seconds

Again, the rules of logs method can be used if preferred.

d) What is the surrounding room temperature?

Surrounding room temperature is 22 °C as this is the constant and is not affected at all by the other parts of the modeled formula.

Example 4

In February 2015, it was reported that by the end of the decade there would be 4 billion smartphones in use.

Given that there were 2 billion in use at the time, what was the expected rate of increase per year? Comment on your answer.

This is a growth of the form $y = ka^x$, where $y = 4$ billion, $k = 2$ billion and $x = 5$.

$$4 = 2a^5$$

$$2 = a^5$$

$$a = \sqrt[5]{2}$$

$$a = 1.148698355$$

This is around a 15% increase per year for the next 5 years.

Your comment should relate back to the context, e.g. 'this might be useful to a smartphone business for forecasting future sales and potential profits and planning business expansion.'

It is clear that there are many different examples, but the general approach is the same.

SUMMARY

- There are many examples of exponential growth and decay.
- They are general of the following forms:

Form	Value of Constant	Growth or Decay	General Solution
$y = a^x$	$a > 1$	growth	use log function
$y = a^x$	$0 < a < 1$	decay	use log function
$y = a^{-x}$	$a > 1$	decay	use log function
$y = e^{kx}$	$k > 0$	growth	use ln function
$y = e^{kx}$	$k < 0$	decay	use ln function

- It is always sensible to consider the answers obtained within context when making comments.
- Remember, ln and e are the inverse of each other and $\ln(e) = 1$.

QUICK TEST

1. If a bank account gives 5% interest, what would be the growth factor in the mathematical model?

2. In the equation for the growth of a population, $N = 2500\,e^{0.042t}$, what is the starting population?

3. Miho invests £10 000 in an account with 4.6% APR.

   a) What is the equation she could use to calculate the value of her investment has as time goes by?

   b) How much would Miho have after 5 years?

4. A pyramid selling scheme requires each person contacted to find five more people. How many 'levels' would it take for the pyramid to exceed 1 million people?

5. A new luxury car costs £3 000 000. Its value depreciates at 8% per year.

   a) What is the equation to model this depreciation and how long would the car take to halve in value?

   b) How much value will be lost between the beginning of the second year and the end of the second year of ownership?

6. Assile has a rechargeable light for his bike. He believes that the time it lasts between full charges halves every 10 months. How long will it last after two years compared to when it was new?

PRACTICE QUESTIONS

1 Henry runs a second-hand CD shop. He sells about 1000 CDs a month.

He needs to sell about 600 a month to break even.

If sales are declining by 10% a year and it is now 1st January 2017, when will Henry stop making a profit on CDs?　　　　**[5 marks]**

2. Assile measures the voltage on his rechargeable battery with time and obtains the following results.

Time (mins)	0	30	60	90	120
Voltage (V)	0	1.5	2.25	2.6	2.8

a) What is the final voltage on the battery?　　　　**[1 mark]**

b) Assile thinks that the voltage on the battery is given by $V = V_0(1 - 2^{-h})$.

What should be used for V_0 and h for the numbers to match up?　　　　**[2 marks]**

c) Assile thinks that 90% of a full charge will be enough.

How long will this take?　　　　**[5 marks]**

3. Cindy has worked out that she has received an average of 4.8% return on her investments over the last five years.

She wants to produce an equation to model the value in the future.

a) What equation could she use?　　　　**[3 marks]**

b) What assumptions are you making?　　　　**[2 marks]**

c) Cindy's initial investment is worth £25 000.

How much profit will she make between years 3 and 4 if she pays tax at a rate of 45%?　　　　**[4 marks]**

acceleration – the rate at which an object changes speed

activity network – a flowchart, read from left to right, that indicates the sequence of activities in a project

activity-on-node network – an activity network that uses a node to show each activity and its duration

AER (annual equivalent rate) – an overall annual rate used to make comparisons between savings accounts only; uses the compound interest formula

affordability – eligibility for a loan or mortgage based on criteria such as income, loan-to-value amount, credit rating and expenses

appreciation – an increase in the value of an asset over time

APR (annual percentage rate) – similar to the AER but is generally used for borrowing, e.g. loans, mortgages and credit cards

arc – the arrows between nodes on an activity-on-node network

assumption – a quantity or relationship that is assumed for the purpose of a model or estimate

asymptote – where the line of a curve gets very close to the x-axis but will never reach a zero value

average acceleration –

$$\text{average acceleration} = \frac{\text{change in speed}}{\text{time taken for change}}$$

average speed – $\text{average speed} = \dfrac{\text{distance travelled}}{\text{time taken}}$

back-to-back stem-and-leaf diagram – two stem-and-leaf diagrams presented back-to-back with the same 'stem', so the data sets can be compared

base 10 – the decimal number system (where the ten digits: 1, 2, 3, 4, 5, 6, 7, 8, 9 and 0 are used to show all numbers)

bias – a tendency either towards or away from a value; unfair

BIDMAS – (or BODMAS) gives the order in which operations should be carried out in a calculation, i.e. brackets, indices, division or multiplication and addition or subtraction

box and whisker plot – a graphical representation of the distribution of a set of data, showing the median, quartiles and extremes

buy rate – how much foreign currency is needed to buy one unit of local currency

census – an official survey of the population of a country in order to find out how many people live there and details such as people's ages and occupations

cluster sample – the population is divided into obvious different (heterogeneous) groups or clusters and a simple random sample is taken from each of the groups

complementary probability – the probability of an event not happening

compound interest – interest is calculated on the investment amount plus any interest previously earned

compound project – a project made up of a series of parts, activities or even smaller projects

confidence interval – the interval within which an unknown parameter of distribution (usually μ) is expected to lie with a given level of confidence

Consumer Price Index (CPI) – measures changes in prices of consumer goods and services purchased by households

continuous data – data that can take any value in a given range, e.g. length or time

contradictory – opposing or conflicting

control measure – a measure put in place to minimise or eliminate a risk

correlation – a relationship between two variables

cost-benefit analysis – the process of quantifying and comparing the benefits and costs of different decisions

credit rating – a measure of how trusted an applicant is to pay back a loan, based on income and past records

critical activities – the activities that take the longest time from start to finish, which would result in an overall delay if they overrun

critical analysis – the process of evaluating and judging

critical path – the path through a network, from start to finish, that takes the longest; delays in any of the activities along this path will result in an overall delay to the completion of the project

critical path analysis – planning complex projects or procedures with reference to a critical path

cubic – an equation containing an x^3 term that produces an S-shaped curve

cumulative frequency graph – an S-shaped curve (ogive) produced by plotting the upper class boundary against the cumulative frequency (the running total)

data – information; facts and statistics collected together for references or analysis

dependent – an outcome that is affected by a previous outcome

dependent (responsive) variable – a variable whose variation depends on that of another, e.g. the number of ice creams sold is dependent on the temperature

depreciation – a decrease in the value of an asset over time

discrete data – data that can only take certain values in a given range, e.g. number of goals scored

distance–time graph – a graph that shows distance travelled from a fixed point over time, where the gradient of the line is the speed

emotive – something that arouses intense feeling

equation – a number sentence where one side is equal to the other

estimate – to calculate an approximate value

evaluating – to draw conclusions about the accuracy, validity, reliability, quality and usefulness of information

event – a particular outcome

exchange rate – the cost of one currency compared to another, e.g. how much of another currency one unit of local currency will buy at a particular time

exhaustive – all possible outcomes are included

expected outcome – the probability of an outcome × the number of trials

expected value – a mean value;
$EV = p_1 v_1 + p_2 v_2 + \dots p_n v_n$

experiment – a set of actions to find the result (outcome) of an activity

experimental probability – the probability as determined by the results of an experiment

exponent – a power or index

exponential – an increase or decrease where the rate of change is expressed by an exponential function, i.e. a function involving a power or index

exponential decay – an exponential function where the exponent is negative, $y = ab^{-x}$

exponential function – a function in which the variable (argument) is the power of a constant, e.g. a^x

exponential growth – an exponential function where the exponent is positive, $y = ab^x$

extrapolation – when estimates lie outside the data set range, based on an assumption that the trend continues outside the data range

fair (unbiased) – all outcomes are equally likely

Fermi estimate – a quick method of estimating a quantity, often used when there is little information available

first quadrant – the area on the top right of a graph, i.e. containing positive values of x and positive values of y

float – float = the latest time – the earliest time – the duration, i.e. the extra time available to complete an activity

fourth quadrant – the area on the bottom right of a graph, i.e. containing positive values of x and negative values of y

frequency density – frequency density is the measure on the y-axis of a histogram; frequency density = $\frac{\text{class frequency}}{\text{class width}}$

Gantt chart (cascade diagram) – a simple diagram that shows the durations and precedents of all the activities in a project with time along the x-axis

geometric mean – the square root of the product of the upper and lower bounds

gradient – the slope of a line;

$$\text{gradient} = \frac{\text{change in } y}{\text{change in } x} \text{ or } \frac{y_2 - y_1}{x_2 - x_1}$$

graphical – a visual representation of data, e.g. a graph

histogram – a chart used to show continuous data, in which the area of each bar is proportional to the frequency of that class

income multiple – the multiple of income that a lender will allow for a loan or income

income tax – a direct percentage tax on a salary or wage (usually monthly)

independent – an outcome or event that is not dependent on another

independent (explanatory) variable – a variable whose variation does not depend on that of another

inflation – the rate of increase in prices for goods and services

intercept – the point where two curves meet or where a curve crosses one of the axes (usually the y-axis)

interpolation – when estimates occur within the data set range

interpolation – to find values between known data points

interquartile range (IQR) – the difference between the lower quartile and the upper quartile, i.e. IQR = $Q_3 - Q_1$

interval error – the range of values (between the upper and lower bounds) in which the precise value of a rounded number could be

inverse – the opposite operation, e.g. multiplication is the inverse of division

linear – describes an equation that produces a straight-line graph

line of best fit – a straight line that best represents the data on a scatter diagram

loan to value (LTV) – the percentage of the sale value of the property for which a mortgage is required or allowed

lower bound – the lower limit of a rounded number

lower quartile (Q_1) – the 25th percentile, i.e. the value $\frac{1}{4}$ or 25% of the way through the data set

maximum point – the value of a function at a certain point, which is greater than or equal to all other local points (the highest point of the curve)

mean ($\bar{x}$) – an average found by dividing the sum of all values by the number of values, i.e. mean = $\frac{\text{sum of all values}}{\text{number of values}}$

median (Q_2) – the middle value in a data set when the data is arranged in numerical order

minimum point – the value of a function at a certain point, which is less than or equal to all other local points (the lowest point of the curve)

mode – the most frequently occurring value in a data set

model – the use of a set of variables and equations to represent a system or real life situation (usually involving simplifications and assumptions), for the purpose of understanding, problem-solving or predicting future outcomes

National Insurance – a contribution paid (by people 16 or over in the UK who are earning above a threshold amount) to qualify for certain benefits, including the state pension

negative argument – a negative variable in a function

negative correlation – a relationship between two variables, where when one variable increases, the other decreases; most data points are in the 2nd and 4th quadrant relative to ($\bar{x}, \bar{y}$)

node – points on an activity-on-node network

normal distribution – when the distribution of a data set can be represented by a bell-shaped curve

notation – the use of symbols to represent variables

outgoings – also called 'expenses'; costs that have to be paid out of the monthly income, e.g. food, utilities, travel, etc.

P(B) – notation for the probability of event B occurring

point estimate – the use of a sample statistic, e.g. the sample mean at a point to represent the population

point of inflexion – the point at which a curve changes direction

population – the entire pool from which a sample is drawn, e.g. all the people living in a town or all the members of a club

population mean (μ) – $\frac{\text{the sum of all population data points}}{\text{total of the population}}$

positive argument – a positive variable in a function

positive correlation – a relationship between two variables, where when one variable increases the other also increases; most data points are in the 3rd and 1st quadrant relative to ($\bar{x}, \bar{y}$)

precedence table – a table that lists the separate activities that need to be completed in a project, including duration and order of precedence

primary data – data collected by you or on your behalf

probability – a measure of how likely it is that an event or outcome will happen

product moment correlation coefficient (pmcc) – a measure of the strength of a correlation; always has a value in the range from −1 to 1

project – a planned enterprise to achieve a particular outcome

quadratic – an equation that contains an unknown term with a power of 2 (a square), e.g. $y = 2x^2 + 3$

qualitative – data that describes a quality or non-numerical aspect of an item or good

quantitative – numerical data obtained by counting or measuring

quota sample – a pre-set number (quota) of representative individuals chosen from a specific subgroup, e.g. 100 females or 100 individuals aged 18–24

random event – an outcome that happens by chance

random sample – a sample selected in a way that ensures each individual or item in the population has an equal chance of being selected

range – the spread of a data set, i.e. range = highest value – lowest value

rate of change – a change in one variable relative to a change in another; given by the gradient of a line, e.g. $\frac{\text{changes in } y}{\text{changes in } x}$

recurrence relation – an equation or relationship that is repeated or reiterated to produce a sequence of values

regression line – a line of best fit with an equation in the form $y = a + bx$ (from $y = mx + c$), where a gives the value for y when $x = 0$, and b gives the change in y for every unit change in x

Retail Price Index (RPI) – a measure of inflation; it measures the change in the cost of a representative sample of retail goods and services

risk – a potential loss or undesirable result associated with an action

sample – a proportion of the population

sample mean ($\bar{x}$) –
$$\frac{\text{the sum of all the sample data points}}{\text{total in the sample}} \text{ or } \bar{x} = \frac{\sum x}{n}$$

sample space – a probability diagram that shows all possible outcomes

sampling – the process of selecting a sample, i.e. a proportion of a population

secondary data – data that comes from other sources, e.g. the internet; the data has been collected by a third party

second quadrant – the area on the top left of a graph, i.e. containing negative values of x and positive values of y

sell rate – how much foreign currency is sold for every one unit of local currency

simple interest – interest is calculated based on the original investment amount

simplification – to simplify a number or relationship for the purpose of a model or estimate

speed–time graph – a graph showing how the speed of an object changes over time, where the gradient of the line is the acceleration

spurious – likely to be false or incorrect

standard deviation (σ) – a 'mean distance' from the mean of a data set; used to measure how spread out the data is

standardised – to convert a normally distributed real life variable to a standard z score for the purpose of analysis

statistic – a calculated numerical value that represents an aspect of the population data

stem-and-leaf diagram – data is displayed in a table in which each data value is split into a 'stem' (often the tens number) and 'leaf' (often the units)

Day 2

Spec Ref.	Learning Aim		Needs work	OK	No Problem
F1.1	substituting numerical values into formulae, spreadsheets and financial expressions	including bank accounts			
F1.2	using conventional notation for priority of operations, including brackets, powers, roots and reciprocals				
F1.3	applying and interpreting limits of accuracy, specifying simple error intervals due to truncation or rounding				
F1.4	finding approximate solutions to problems in financial contexts				
F2.1	interpreting percentages and percentage changes as a fraction or a decimal and interpreting these multiplicatively				
F2.2	expressing one quantity as a percentage of another				
F2.3	comparing two quantities using percentages				
F2.4	working with percentages over 100%				
F2.5	solving problems involving percentage change	including percentage increase /decrease and original value problems including simple and compound interest			
F3.1	simple and compound interest	Annual equivalent rate (AER)			
F3.2	savings and investments				
F4.1	student loans and mortgages	Annual percentage rate (APR)			
F5.1	graphical representation	plotting points to create graphs and interpreting results from graphs in financial contexts			

Day 2 continued

F6.1	income tax, National Insurance, Value Added Tax (VAT)				
F7.1	the effect of inflation	Retail Price Index (RPI), Consumer Price Index (CPI)			
F7.2	setting up, solving and interpreting the solutions to financial problems, including those that involve compound interest using iterative methods				
F7.3	Currency exchange rates including commission				
F7.4	budgeting				

Day 3

Spec Ref.	Learning Aim		Needs work	OK	No Problem
E1.1	representing a situation mathematically, making assumptions and simplifications	tackling 'open' problems with no obvious single approach or 'correct' answer			
E1.2	selecting and using appropriate mathematical techniques for problems and situations				
E1.3	interpreting results in the context of a given problem				
E1.4	evaluating methods and solutions and how they have been affected by the assumptions made				
E2.1	making fast, rough estimates of quantities which are difficult or impossible to measure directly				

Day 4

Spec Ref.	Learning Aim	Needs work	OK	No Problem
C1.1	criticising the arguments of others			
C2.1	summarising and report writing			
C3.1	comparing results from a model with real data			
C3.2	critical analysis of data quoted in media, political campaigns, marketing, etc.			

Day 5 Option 1

Spec Ref.	Learning Aim		Needs work	OK	No Problem
S1.1	knowledge that the normal distribution is a symmetrical distribution and that the area underneath the normal 'bell' shaped curve represents probability	knowledge that approximately $\frac{2}{3}$ of observations lie within 1 standard deviation of the mean and that approximately 95% of observations lie within 2 standard deviations of the mean			
S2.1	use of the notation N(μ, σ^2) to describe a normal distribution in terms of mean and standard deviation	use of the notation $N(0, 1)$ for the standardised normal distribution with mean = 0 and standard deviation = 1			
S3.1	using a calculator or tables to find probabilities for normally distributed data with known mean and standard deviation	finding an unknown mean or standard deviation by making use of percentage points will not be required			

Day 6 Option 1

Spec Ref.	Learning Aim		Needs work	OK	No Problem
S4.1	understanding what is meant by the term 'population' in statistical terms				
S4.2	developing ideas of sampling to include the concept of a simple random sample from a population				
S5.1	knowing that the mean of a sample is called a 'point estimate' for the mean of the population	appreciating that accuracy is likely to be improved by increasing the sample size			
S6.1	confidence intervals for the mean of a normally distributed population of known variance using $\frac{\sigma^2}{n}$	confidence intervals will always be symmetrical the confidence level required and the sample size will always be stated			

Day 7 Option 1

Spec Ref.	Learning Aim		Needs work	OK	No Problem
S7.1	recognising when pairs of data are uncorrelated, correlated, strongly correlated, positively correlated and negatively correlated				
S7.2	appreciating that correlation does not necessarily imply causation				
S7.3	understanding the idea of an outlier	identifying and understanding outliers and make decisions whether or not to include them when drawing a line of best fit			
S8.1	understanding that the strength of correlation is given by the pmcc				
S8.2	understanding that pmcc always has a value in the range from −1 to +1				
S8.3	appreciating the significance of a positive, zero or negative value of pmcc in terms of correlation of data				
S9.1	the plotting of data pairs on scatter diagrams and the drawing, by eye, of a line of best fit through the mean point	the idea of residuals will not be required			
S9.2	understanding the concept of a regression line				
S9.3	plotting a regression line from its equation				
S9.4	using interpolation with regression lines to make predictions				
S9.5	understanding the potential problems of extrapolation				
S10.1	where raw data is given, you will be expected to use a calculator to calculate the pmcc and the equation of the regression line	calculations from grouped data will not be required			

Day 5 Option 2

Spec Ref.	Learning Aim	Needs work	OK	No Problem
R1.1	representing compound projects by activity networks			
R1.2	activity-on-node representation will be used			
R2.1	using early and late time algorithms to identify critical activities and find the critical path(s)			
R3.1	using Gantt charts (cascade diagram) to present project activities			

Day 6 Option 2

Spec Ref.	Learning Aim		Needs work	OK	No Problem
R4.1	understanding that uncertain outcomes can be modelled as random events with estimated probabilities	knowing that the probabilities of an exhaustive set of outcomes have a sum of one			
R4.2	applying ideas of randomness, fairness and equally likely events to calculate expected outcomes				
R5.1	understanding and applying Venn diagrams and simple tree diagrams	• understanding that $P(A)$ means the probability of event A • understanding that $P(A')$ means the probability of not event A • understanding that $P(A \cup B)$ means the probability of event A or B or both • understanding that $P(A \cap B)$ means the probability of event A and B			
R6.1	calculating the probability of combined events: • both A and B • neither A nor B • either A or B (or both)	to include independent and dependent events			
R7.1	calculating the expected value of quantities such as financial loss or gain				

Day 7 Option 2

Spec Ref.	Learning Aim		Needs work	OK	No Problem
R8.1	understanding that many decisions have to be made when outcomes cannot be predicted with certainty				
R9.1	understanding that the actions that can be taken to reduce or prevent specific risks may have their own costs	including the costs and benefits of insurance			
R10.1	using probabilities to calculate expected values of costs and benefits of decisions	other factors must be considered, for example: • the regulatory framework (e.g. compulsory insurance) • minimising the maximum possible loss			
R10.2	understanding that calculating an expected value is an important part of such decision making				

Day 5 Option 3

Spec Ref.	Learning Aim		Needs work	OK	No Problem
G1.1	sketching and plotting curves defined by simple equations	knowing the shapes of the graphs of linear, quadratic, cubic and exponential functions will be expected			
G2.1	plotting and interpreting graphs (including exponential graphs) in real contexts, to find approximate solutions to problems	including understanding the potential problems of extrapolation			
G2.2	interpreting the solutions of equations as the intersection points of graphs and vice versa				

Day 6 Option 3

Spec Ref.	Learning Aim		Needs work	OK	No Problem
G3.1	interpreting the gradient of a straight line graph as a rate of change				
G3.2	interpreting the gradient at a point on a curve as an instantaneous rate of change	understanding that some maximum and minimum points on curves occur where the gradient is zero			
G3.3	estimating rates of change for functions from their graphs				
G4.1	knowing that the average speed of an object during a particular period of time is given by $\frac{\text{distance travelled}}{\text{time taken}}$				
G5.1	knowing that the gradient of a distance–time graph represents speed and that the gradient of a velocity–time graph represents acceleration				

Day 7 Option 3

Spec Ref.	Learning Aim		Needs work	OK	No Problem
G6.1	using a calculator to find values of function a^x	the laws of logarithms will not be required			
G6.2	using a calculator log function to solve equations of the form $a^x = b$ and $e^{kx} = b$				
G7.1	understanding that e has been chosen as the standard base for exponential functions	knowing that the gradient at any point on the graph of $y = e^x$ is equal to the y value of that point			
G8.1	formulating and using equations of the form $y = Ca^x$ and $y = Ce^{kx}$				
G8.2	using exponential functions to model growth and decay in various contexts				

Table 1 – Normal Distribution Function

The table gives the probability, p, that a normally distributed random variable Z, with mean = 0 and variance = 1, is less than or equal to z.

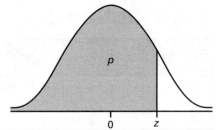

z	0.00	0.01	0.02	0.03	0.04	0.05	0.06	0.07	0.08	0.09	z
0.0	0.50000	0.50399	0.50798	0.51197	0.51595	0.51994	0.52392	0.52790	0.53188	0.53586	0.0
0.1	0.53983	0.54380	0.54776	0.55172	0.55567	0.55962	0.56356	0.56749	0.57142	0.57535	0.1
0.2	0.57926	0.58317	0.58706	0.59095	0.59483	0.59871	0.60257	0.60642	0.61026	0.61409	0.2
0.3	0.61791	0.62172	0.62552	0.62930	0.63307	0.63683	0.64058	0.64431	0.64803	0.65173	0.3
0.4	0.65542	0.65910	0.66276	0.66640	0.67003	0.67364	0.67724	0.68082	0.68439	0.68793	0.4
0.5	0.69146	0.69497	0.69847	0.70194	0.70540	0.70884	0.71226	0.71566	0.71904	0.72240	0.5
0.6	0.72575	0.72907	0.73237	0.73565	0.73891	0.74215	0.74537	0.74857	0.75175	0.75490	0.6
0.7	0.75804	0.76115	0.76424	0.76730	0.77035	0.77337	0.77637	0.77935	0.78230	0.78524	0.7
0.8	0.78814	0.79103	0.79389	0.79673	0.79955	0.80234	0.80511	0.80785	0.81057	0.81327	0.8
0.9	0.81594	0.81859	0.82121	0.82381	0.82639	0.82894	0.83147	0.83398	0.83646	0.83891	0.9
1.0	0.84134	0.84375	0.84614	0.84849	0.85083	0.85314	0.85543	0.85769	0.85993	0.86214	1.0
1.1	0.86433	0.86650	0.86864	0.87076	0.87286	0.87493	0.87698	0.87900	0.88100	0.88298	1.1
1.2	0.88493	0.88686	0.88877	0.89065	0.89251	0.89435	0.89617	0.89796	0.89973	0.90147	1.2
1.3	0.90320	0.90490	0.90658	0.90824	0.90988	0.91149	0.91309	0.91466	0.91621	0.91774	1.3
1.4	0.91924	0.92073	0.92220	0.92364	0.92507	0.92647	0.92785	0.92922	0.93056	0.93189	1.4
1.5	0.93319	0.93448	0.93574	0.93699	0.93822	0.93943	0.94062	0.94179	0.94295	0.94408	1.5
1.6	0.94520	0.94630	0.94738	0.94845	0.94950	0.95053	0.95154	0.95254	0.95352	0.95449	1.6
1.7	0.95543	0.95637	0.95728	0.95818	0.95907	0.95994	0.96080	0.96164	0.96246	0.96327	1.7
1.8	0.96407	0.96485	0.96562	0.96638	0.96712	0.96784	0.96856	0.96926	0.96995	0.97062	1.8
1.9	0.97128	0.97193	0.97257	0.97320	0.97381	0.97441	0.97500	0.97558	0.97615	0.97670	1.9
2.0	0.97725	0.97778	0.97831	0.97882	0.97932	0.97982	0.98030	0.98077	0.98124	0.98169	2.0
2.1	0.98214	0.98257	0.98300	0.98341	0.98382	0.98422	0.98461	0.98500	0.98537	0.98574	2.1
2.2	0.98610	0.98645	0.98679	0.98713	0.98745	0.98778	0.98809	0.98840	0.98870	0.98899	2.2
2.3	0.98928	0.98956	0.98983	0.99010	0.99036	0.99061	0.99086	0.99111	0.99134	0.99158	2.3
2.4	0.99180	0.99202	0.99224	0.99245	0.99266	0.99286	0.99305	0.99324	0.99343	0.99361	2.4
2.5	0.99379	0.99396	0.99413	0.99430	0.99446	0.99461	0.99477	0.99492	0.99506	0.99520	2.5
2.6	0.99534	0.99547	0.99560	0.99573	0.99585	0.99598	0.99609	0.99621	0.99632	0.99643	2.6
2.7	0.99653	0.99664	0.99674	0.99683	0.99693	0.99702	0.99711	0.99720	0.99728	0.99736	2.7
2.8	0.99744	0.99752	0.99760	0.99767	0.99774	0.99781	0.99788	0.99795	0.99801	0.99807	2.8
2.9	0.99813	0.99819	0.99825	0.99831	0.99836	0.99841	0.99846	0.99851	0.99856	0.99861	2.9
3.0	0.99865	0.99869	0.99874	0.99878	0.99882	0.99886	0.99889	0.99893	0.99896	0.99900	3.0
3.1	0.99903	0.99906	0.99910	0.99913	0.99916	0.99918	0.99921	0.99924	0.99926	0.99929	3.1
3.2	0.99931	0.99934	0.99936	0.99938	0.99940	0.99942	0.99944	0.99946	0.99948	0.99950	3.2
3.3	0.99952	0.99953	0.99955	0.99957	0.99958	0.99960	0.99961	0.99962	0.99964	0.99965	3.3
3.4	0.99966	0.99968	0.99969	0.99970	0.99971	0.99972	0.99973	0.99974	0.99975	0.99976	3.4
3.5	0.99977	0.99978	0.99978	0.99979	0.99980	0.99981	0.99981	0.99982	0.99983	0.99983	3.5
3.6	0.99984	0.99985	0.99985	0.99986	0.99986	0.99987	0.99987	0.99988	0.99988	0.99989	3.6
3.7	0.99989	0.99990	0.99990	0.99990	0.99991	0.99991	0.99992	0.99992	0.99992	0.99992	3.7
3.8	0.99993	0.99993	0.99993	0.99994	0.99994	0.99994	0.99994	0.99995	0.99995	0.99995	3.8
3.9	0.99995	0.99995	0.99996	0.99996	0.99996	0.99996	0.99996	0.99996	0.99997	0.99997	3.9

Table 2 – Percentage Points of the Normal Distribution

The table gives the values of z satisfying $P\,(Z \le z) = p$, where Z is the normally distributed random variable with mean = 0 and variance = 1.

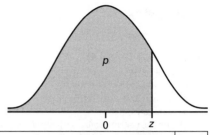

p	0.00	0.01	0.02	0.03	0.04	0.05	0.06	0.07	0.08	0.09	p
0.5	0.0000	0.0251	0.0502	0.0753	0.1004	0.1257	0.1510	0.1764	0.2019	0.2275	0.5
0.6	0.2533	0.2793	0.3055	0.3319	0.3585	0.3853	0.4125	0.4399	0.4677	0.4958	0.6
0.7	0.5244	0.5534	0.5828	0.6128	0.6433	0.6745	0.7063	0.7388	0.7722	0.8064	0.7
0.8	0.8416	0.8779	0.9154	0.9542	0.9945	1.0364	1.0803	1.1264	1.1750	1.2265	0.8
0.9	1.2816	1.3408	1.4051	1.4758	1.5548	1.6449	1.7507	1.8808	2.0537	2.3263	0.9
p	0.000	0.001	0.002	0.003	0.004	0.005	0.006	0.007	0.008	0.009	p
0.95	1.6449	1.6546	1.6646	1.6747	1.6849	1.6954	1.7060	1.7169	1.7279	1.7392	0.95
0.96	1.7507	1.7624	1.7744	1.7866	1.7991	1.8119	1.8250	1.8384	1.8522	1.8663	0.96
0.97	1.8808	1.8957	1.9110	1.9268	1.9431	1.9600	1.9774	1.9954	2.0141	2.0335	0.97
0.98	2.0537	2.0749	2.0969	2.1201	2.1444	2.1701	2.1973	2.2262	2.2571	2.2904	0.98
0.99	2.3263	2.3656	2.4089	2.4573	2.5121	2.5758	2.6521	2.7478	2.8782	3.0902	0.99

Answers

Answers

Types of Data
QUICK TEST (Page 5)
1. a) qualitative
   b) quantitative – continuous
   c) quantitative – discrete
   d) qualitative
   e) either or both: qualitative if replies are 'likely' or 'unlikely'; quantitative if a calculated percentage based on performance in mock exams/tests
   f) quantitative – continuous
2. a) **Any three examples of qualitative data,** e.g. type of material (e.g. steel, glass, bricks, paint, etc.); type of furnishings (e.g. desks, seating, decorations, etc.); colour of materials/furnishings.
   b) **Any three examples of quantitative data (with at least one discrete example and one continuous example), e.g. discrete: number of items used** (e.g. panes of glass); continuous: time taken for different parts of construction process; dimensions of building; length/height/weight of building materials/furniture

PRACTICE QUESTIONS (Page 5)
1. quantitative [1]; discrete [1]

Collecting and Sampling Data
QUICK TEST (Page 8)
1. a) primary
   b) secondary
   c) primary
   d) secondary
2. a) They should use secondary data; primary research would be very costly and, if the journalist is not a medically trained expert, conclusions about effectiveness would be questionable (or even biased if the sole decider); using secondary data from research already carried out would be less costly and time consuming
   b) A stratified random sample to get a fair representation of the different age groups

PRACTICE QUESTIONS (Page 8)
1. a) Age group '51+' [1]; contains 55% females, so should have 6 representatives ($0.55 \times 10 = 5.53 = 6$ to the nearest whole number) [1]
   b) A stratified random sample of 30 with the number chosen from each group proportionate to the size of the group [1]; Age 18–25 = 10 (5M, 5F) [1]; Age 26–50 = 6 ($\frac{59}{300} \times 30$) (3M, 3F) [1]; Age 51+ = 14 ($\frac{144}{300} \times 30$) (6M, 8F) [1]
2. a) Choose two members at random [1]; from each age group [1]
   b) i) Random sample: assign numbers 1 to 20 to members of the cooperative [1]; using the random number table, work down the columns (left to right) or across the rows (top to bottom) selecting the first six numbers between 1 and 20 (inclusive and ignoring repeats) [1]; column option gives 1, 19, 10, 8, 15 and 18 / row option gives 8, 1, 18, 15, 2 and 19 [1]
   ii) Stratified sample: Age 18–35 = 2 members ($\frac{2}{20} \times 6$) [1]; Age 36–50 = 3 members ($\frac{9}{20} \times 6$) [1]; Age 51–65 = 1 member ($\frac{4}{20} \times 6$) [1]; numbers need to be assigned to each person and the sample from each group should be chosen randomly [1]
3. a) Executive = 2 ($\frac{12}{150} \times 21$); Admin = 3 ($\frac{20}{150} \times 21$) [1]; Supervisors = 1 ($\frac{10}{150} \times 21$) [1]; IT Support = 1 ($\frac{6}{150} \times 21$) [1]; Manual Staff = 14 ($\frac{102}{150} \times 21$) [1]

   b) Manual Staff = 10 = 68% ($\frac{102}{150} \times 100$) [1]; 100% = $\frac{10}{68} \times 100 = 14.71$, so 15 in sample [1] OR $\frac{102}{150} \times n = 10$ [1]; $n = \frac{10}{0.68} = 14.71$, so 15 in sample [1]

Representing Data Numerically
QUICK TEST (Page 12)
1. a) Mean = $\frac{(12 + 12 + 14 + 15 + 15 + 15 + 17)}{7} = \frac{100}{7} = 14.29$ (to 2 dp)
   b) Mode = 15
   c) Median = 15
2. a) Range = 17 – 12 = 5
   b) IQR = 15 – 12 = 3
   c) SD = 1.665986
3. IQR involves the middle 50% of the data
4. $\bar{x} = \frac{((17 \times 1) + (33 \times 2) + (26 \times 3) + (14 \times 4) + (6 \times 5) + (4 \times 6))}{100} = \frac{271}{100} = 2.71$

   $\sigma = \sqrt{\frac{(17 \times 1^2 + 33 \times 2^2 + 26 \times 3^2 + 14 \times 4^2 + 6 \times 5^2 + 4 \times 6^2)}{100} - 2.71} = 1.297$

PRACTICE QUESTIONS (Page 13)
1. 2.5 SD = 85 – 40 = 45% [1]; so, 1 SD = $\frac{45}{2.5} = 18\%$ [1]
2. 3 SD would mean scores of 1.8 – (3 × 0.78) = –0.54 at the lower end [1]; and 1.8 + (3 × 0.78) = 4.14 at the upper end [1]; so it is possible to have a number of children more than 3 SD at the upper end [1]; but not at the lower end (this would read as zero) [1]
3. a) Machine A: $\bar{x} = \frac{13.46}{6} = 2.24$ (to 2 dp) [1]; $\sigma = 0.0476\ldots$ for $n - 1$ used [1]; Machine B: $\bar{x} = \frac{23.78}{9} = 2.64$ (to 2 dp) [1]; $\sigma = 0.764\ldots$ [1]
   b) Machine A is more consistent [1]; as it has a lower standard deviation (and a larger sample was used so the values are likely to be more reliable) [1]
4. a) Data set is secondary (from another source) [1]; quantitative and continuous [1]
   b) Mean = $\frac{243.52}{10} = 24.35$ [1]; SD = 2.78 [1]
   c) **Any two from:** No, because the given data set is small [1]; not randomly selected [1]; unlikely to be representative [1]

Representing Data in Diagrams
QUICK TEST (Page 16)
1. A back-to-back stem-and-leaf diagram compares two sets of data that have similar characteristics; a normal stem-and-leaf diagram deals the distribution of just one data set
2. Whiskers, which extend from the box, usually show the lowest score (on the left) and maximum score on the right; the box shows the lower quartile, median and upper quartile (reading left to right)
3. A running total of scores up to a certain point (usually the end of a class interval)
4. The areas of the bars represent the frequency of each class or group

PRACTICE QUESTIONS (Page 17)
1. a) 1 mark for a correct stem and leaf diagram [1]; 1 mark for a correct key, e.g. 5|01 = 501 m [1]

Stem	Leaf
4	50, 52, 52, 54, 82, 86
5	01, 04, 05, 08, 72
6	58,

   b) 572 m [1]
   c) 658 – 450 = 208 m [1]
   d) 2 (at 452 m) [1]
   e) 508 – 504 = 4 m [1]
   f) Mean = $\frac{(450 + 452 + 452 + 454 + 482 + 486 + 501 + 504 + 505 + 508 + 572 + 658)}{12}$ [1]; = 502 m [1]

2. **a) i)** A horizontal line should be drawn across at $n = 60$ from the axis to the graph **[1]**; a vertical line should be drawn down from this point to the 'Test score' axis giving a reading: median (Q_2) = 53 **[1]**
   ii) Using the same method for part a) at $1/4n$ to give Q_1 = 45 and at $3/4n$ to give Q_3 = 67 **[1]**; IQR = 67 − 45 = 22 **[1]**
   b) 40% of 120 = 48, so you are looking at 72 to 120 on the cumulative frequency scale **[1]**; this gives a mark of 54 or above **[1]**

Numerical Calculations
QUICK TEST (Page 19)
1. Brackets; Indices; Multiplications or Division; Addition or Subtraction
2. Multiplication (the value in cell E3 is to be multiplied by the value in cell D2)
3. When rounding, the final digit might need to be changed up or down to give the number to the nearest unit, 10, 100, etc.; truncating means to cut the number off at a particular point without rounding

PRACTICE QUESTIONS (Page 19)
1. Real revenue = 333 × £90.45 = £30 119.85 **[1]**; £30 119.85 − £30 000 = £119.85, percentage error = $\frac{119.85}{30\,000}$ **[1]**; = 0.3995% **[1]**
2. **a)** = B2+D2 **[1]**
   b) =SUM(D2:D4) **[1]**
   c) = 1000 × $(1.05)^3$ **[1]**

Percentages
QUICK TEST (Page 21)
1. $\frac{9}{20}$; 0.45
2. £331.52; £382.28
3. 32.609%
4. Shop A (Shop A is 12.121% and Shop B is 10.667% to 3 decimal places)
5. **a)** 145%
   b) 267%
6. £450.07 (after increase: £504)
7. £7000

PRACTICE QUESTIONS (Page 21)
1. **a)** $\frac{215}{(15 + 1750 + 35)} \times 100 = 10.75\%$ **[1]**
   b) Drink A = 10.75% lemon juice (as above) and Drink B = $\frac{80}{(80 + 500 + 20)}$ = 13.33% **[1]**; so B contains the greatest percentage of lemon juice **[1]**
   c) $\frac{(215 + 80)}{(215 + 1750 + 35 + 80 + 500 + 20)} \times 100$ **[1]**; = 11.346% **[1]**
   d) Cost of lemon juice = $\frac{£0.20}{100} \times 215$ = £0.43, cost of water = $\frac{£0.40}{1000} \times 1750$ = £0.70, cost of sugar syrup = £0.17 **[1]**; total cost (2000 ml) = £1.30 **[1]**; cost for 100 litres: need 50 lots, so 50 × £1.30 = £65 OR $\frac{£1.30}{2} \times 100 = £65$ **[1]**
   e) Cost of 1 litre (100%) = $\frac{1.30}{2}$ = £0.65 **[1]**; selling price for 30% profit = £0.65 × 1.30 = £0.845 or 85p **[1]**
2. Antenna: $\frac{£12.99}{87} \times 100$ = £14.93 **[1]**; Mobile: $\frac{£49.99}{47} \times 100$ = £106.36 **[1]**; Gaming Laptop: $\frac{£859.99}{57\frac{1}{3}} \times 100$ **[1]**; = £1499.98 **[1]**

Interest Rates
QUICK TEST (Page 27)
1. Simple interest is based on the original investment and produces the same amount or earnings every year/period; compound interest is where interest is earned on the interest earned from previous years/periods as well as the original investment

2. AER is the annual equivalent; it is usually used for savings; APR is the annual percentage rate; it is usually used for loans or mortgages.
3. **a)** £3000 × $(1.03)^5$ = £3477.82
   b) £3000 × $(1.0025)^{60}$ = £3484.85
4. Course fees and maintenance costs (e.g. rent, food and utility bills)
5. A mortgage is a loan to buy property; affordability is usually dependent on income (multiple), normal monthly expenses (excluding rent), LTV and credit rating
6. The LTV (loan to value) is the proportion of the actual property value that the mortgage is required for
7. A repeated process or formula

PRACTICE QUESTIONS (Page 27)
1. £3000 × $(1.03)^t$ = £4000, $(1.03)^t = \frac{£4000}{£3000}$ = 1.333… **[1]**; using trial and improvement, if t = 9, $(1.03)^9$ = 1.30477… and if t = 10, $(1.03)^{10}$ = 1.3439… **[1]**; so the investment will exceed £4000 at 10 years **[1]**
2.

Year	Outstanding Loan Balance Year Begin	Max Interest (3%)	Income	Income Above £21 000	Annual Payment (9% of Income Above £21 000)	Outstanding Balance Year End
1	£25 000.00	£750.00	£19 000.00	£0.00	£0.00	£25 750.00
2	£25 750.00	£772.50	£19 950.00	£0.00	£0.00	£26 522.50
3	£26 522.50	£795.68	£20 947.50	£0.00	£0.00	£27 318.18
4	£27 318.18	£819.55	£21 994.88	£994.88	£89.54	£28 048.18
5	£28 048.18	£841.45	£23 094.62	£2094.62	£188.52	£28 701.11

Repayments start in Year 4 **[1]**; supported by calculations similar to table above **[1]**; monthly payment = $\frac{£89.54}{12}$ = £7.46 **[1]**

Other Financial Aspects
QUICK TEST (Page 30)
1. Income tax is a direct tax based on a percentage of money earned; £11 200 − £11 000 = £200, income tax = £200 × 0.2 = £40
2. Monthly maximum = £672, so weekly maximum = $\frac{(£672 \times 12)}{52}$ = £155.08
3. £12 000 × 0.20 = £2400
4. Over 100 000
5. The buy rate is how much foreign currency is needed to buy one unit of local currency; the sell rate is how much foreign currency is sold for every unit of local currency
6. $145
7. When expenses and income are equal
8. Any graph can be used, but often data is presented in a bar chart, pie chart or line graph

PRACTICE QUESTIONS (Page 31)
1. **a)** Taxable income = £48 000 − £11 000 = £37 000 **[1]**; tax @ 20% on first £32 000 = £32 000 × 0.2 = £6400, tax @ 40% on balance = £5000 × 0.4 = £2000 **[1]**; total income tax per year = £8400 **[1]**
   b) Percentage non-taxed income = $\frac{11}{48} \times 100$ = 22.9% **[1]**
   c) Flat rate tax = $\frac{8400}{48\,000} \times 100$ = 17.5% **[1]**
2. £4500 = 120%, so 20% = $\frac{£4500}{120} \times 20$ **[1]**; = £750 **[1]**
3. **a)** $1.15 × 1000 **[1]**; = $1150 **[1]**
   b) Mid-rate = $\frac{(\$1.22 + \$1.55)}{2}$ = $1.185 **[1]**; percentage profit on sell rate = $\frac{(1.185 - 1.115)}{1.185}$ **[1]**; = 2.95% or close to 3% **[1]**

4. Converting all to US$ gives Canada at $4.60 **[1]**; US at $5.04 and UK at $3.94 **[1]**; the US is the most expensive **[1]** (Accept alternative answers that correctly convert all prices into Can$ or GB£ for comparison)
5. £540 = $A \times (1.02)^{10}$, so $A = \frac{£540}{(1.02)^{10}}$ **[1]**; = £442.99 **[1]**
6. **Any three from:** total spending has been above revenue since about the year 2000/2001 **[1]**; biggest gap in spending over revenue was around 2010/2011 **[1]**; this gap was about (45 − 36 =) 9% **[1]**; biggest gap in revenue over expenditure was around 1991/1992 **[1]**; lowest spending was around 1991 at about 32% GDP **[1]** (accept any other sensible answer based on the data shown)

Using Models

QUICK TEST (Page 34)
Answers may vary.
1. Amount of food per day (could be per person or per family); if this is a mass then it needs to be converted to volume; number of days in a year; shape of pile, e.g. cone with radius same as the height
2. The percentage of people who commute to work, e.g. 50% of the world; number of working days in a year, e.g. 250; number of years worked, e.g. 50 (start work at 18 and retire about 68); time spent travelling to work (doubled for the return journey)
3. Population of Birmingham; percentage of non-school-age children; percentage not looked after by family; number of children looked after by individual or institution
4. Number of books; time to read a book; number of hours available to read per day
5. Model the body as a series of cylinders; length and width of each cylinder
6. Number of days in school year; number of hours in school day; number of years at school and college/university (what percentage continue in higher education?)
7. Number of flats; average water use per household
8. Length of M25 (assume a circle with a certain radius); average speed (could be speed limit or take account of traffic jams)
9. Estimate of size of Earth (assume to be a sphere); estimate of density to get mass; velocity (estimate distance from sun and time to complete one revolution, i.e. a year; assume that the orbit is a circle)

PRACTICE QUESTIONS (Page 35)
Accept any reasonable alternative assumptions and estimates.
1. Correct units used: litres or cubic metres **[1]**; daily amount of 1–2 litres **[1]**; 1.5 × 365 = 550 litres for yearly amount **[1]**; lifespan of 75 years **[1]**; 75 × 550 = around 40 000 litres **[1]** (accept any answer between 20 000 and 60 000 litres)
2. Assume a diamond shape **[1]**; 40 km × 30 km **[1]**; gives 600 km² area **[1]**; can fit 10 people in each m² **[1]**; 600 km² = 600 000 000 m² **[1]**; can fit 10 × 600 000 000 = 6 billion people **[1]**; world population more than 6 billion **[1]**; conclude: no, not possible **[1]**
3. Average car drives 5000 miles per year **[1]**; average fuel consumption 40 miles per gallon **[1]**; gallons per year = $\frac{5000}{40}$ = 125 gallons **[1]**; convert gallons to litres = 125 × 4.5 = 560 litres **[1]**; cost per litre = £1.10 per litre **[1]**; cost per car = 560 × 1.1 = £620 **[1]**; percentage paid in tax, 60%, so 620 × 0.6 = £370 per car **[1]**; number of cars in UK = 25 million **[1]**; total tax paid = 25 000 000 × £370 = £9.3 billion **[1]**
4. 500 people on train (maximum capacity 750) **[1]**; 2 people on step per second **[1]**; $\frac{500}{2}$ = 250 seconds if just one escalator **[1]**; using iteration: $\frac{500}{4}$ = 125, $\frac{500}{6}$ = 83, $\frac{500}{8}$ = 63, $\frac{500}{10}$ = 50 **[1]**; 5 escalators are needed **[1]**

Interpreting and Evaluating Results

QUICK TEST (Page 38)
1. Probably not, as location can influence price; it might be possible to use the same model and change some of the values, e.g. the cost per square metre
2. Assuming that the proportions are the same, the volume would depend on the dimension cubed, so 8 times as much, i.e. 8 litres
3. **a)** Length of arm; player's strength; material of racket; length of racket; material of ball; temperature of ball; air temperature and humidity, etc.
   b) Given the restrictions on the material and dimensions of ball and racket in the sport, probably the strength and size of the player
4. As the player repeats the exercise they will probably improve and the probability will change with time
5. Yes, for almost all models as the circumference around the poles is 40 007 km and around the equator 40 075 km.
6. The forest might not contain any of the tree species that the beetle attacks
7. Assuming that profit is related to the revenue, the revenue itself will be a product of the sale price multiplied by the number sold; if the price is very small, but the sales high, the revenue will still be small; similarly, if the price is very high the sales will be very low and the revenue will be low; somewhere between these there will be an optimum price
8. No, it would depend on the type of tea, the shape of the mug, the ambient temperature, if there is any wind, etc.

PRACTICE QUESTIONS (Page 39)
Accept any reasonable alternative assumptions and estimates.
1. Assume that all the patients visit the mid-point number of times, e.g. 5 patients visit 2.5 times **[1]**; mean = $\frac{(5 \times 2.5 + 47 \times 7.5 + 11 \times 12.5)}{63}$ **[1]**; = $\frac{502.5}{63}$ = 7.98 **[1]**; = 8 visits **[1]**
2. Assume that there is a fixed cost and a cost per mile $C = F + Md$ **[1]**; this gives the fixed cost (F) as £2.50 **[1]**; and the cost per mile (M) as £2.00 **[1]**; assume an average speed in town of 15 miles per hour **[1]**; therefore, 7.5 miles in 30 minutes **[1]**; $C = 2.5 + 2 \times 7.5$ **[1]**; = £17.50 **[1]**
3. Assume 10% of the world buys cola **[1]**; say 1 billion **[1]**; height of bottle is about 20 cm **[1]**; diameter is about 7 cm **[1]**; assumed bottles are packed in a cuboid **[1]**; 20 × 7 × 7 = about 1000 cm³ = 0.001 m³ **[1]**; 1 billion × 0.001 **[1]**; = 1 million cubic meters (About the volume of the Empire State Building!) **[1]**
4. Assume river is a cuboid 100 m wide and 1 km long **[1]**; the mean depth of additional water is 2 m **[1]**; volume of 'raised' water is 100 × 1000 × 4 = 2 × 10⁵ m³ **[1]**; = 4 × 10⁵ kg **[1]**; energy available is 4 × 10⁵ × 9.81 × 2 = 7.85 million Joules **[1]**; assume 10% efficient, **[1]**; to gives 0.8 million Joules **[1]**; twice a day, therefore about 1.5 million Joules **[1]**

Fermi Estimates

QUICK TEST (Page 41)
1. The upper or lower limit for a value
2. The nth root of the product of n numbers, e.g. the square root of two numbers multiplied together
3. A rough estimate (named after the physicist, Enrico Fermi) often used when there is very little information available
4. Dividing into smaller parts; comparing to known quantities; using upper and lower bounds; simplifying values, shapes, etc.
5. 200 miles and 100 000 miles (Accept any other sensible answer)
6. 30 g (This is the recommended maximum)

7. 8 hours a day, i.e. one third, one third of a lifetime = 25 years OR $8 \times 365 \times 75 \approx 220\,000$ hours

8. Smaller than London, so 3 million (about 2.34 million in 2014)

9. 20 000 people, 1 in 10 buys a sausage roll, so 2 000

10. 10 million children, £5 a week, 52 weeks a year $\approx$ 2.5 billion pounds

PRACTICE QUESTIONS (Page 41)

Accept any reasonable alternative assumptions and estimates.

1. Assume a difference of £10 000 pounds [1]; for 40 years [1]; to gives £400 000 [1]

2. 50 books per shelf [1]; 6 shelves per unit [1]; 100 units in the library [1]; this gives 30 000 books [1]; 2 minutes per page [1]; 150 pages [1]; so 5 hours per book [1]; $30\,000 \times 5 = 150\,000$ hours [1]

3. 50 metres long [1]; 25 metres wide [1]; 2 meters deep [1]; = 2500 m^3 [1]; = 2 500 000 litres [1]; 1 litre every 5 seconds (imagine filling a litre bottle from the tap) [1]; $2\,500\,000 \times 5 = 12\,500\,000$ seconds [1]; about 3500 hours [1]

4. Assume seawater is 3% salt [1]; 0.03 g/cm^3 is salt [1]; a person might use 3 g per day [1]; therefore, 100 cm^3 (or milliltres) or 0.1 litres [1]; assume population of Dubai is 3 million [1]; therefore, $3\,000\,000 \times 0.1 = 300\,000$ litres per day [1]

5. Population of UK is 70 million [1]; 10% buy one disposable cup per day [1]; gives 7 million [1]

Criticising the Arguments of Others

QUICK TEST (Page 44)

1. The percentages do not add up to 100%

2. There is no scale (vertical axis) for either value; the relative changes appear to be the same when they are not

3. Picking a small section of a long-term trend may give a false impression; the information is not completely clear
The questions would influence the results of any poll as they 'lead' the respondent to a particular answer, so the data would be biased

4. Car accidents cause bird attacks; bird attacks cause car accidents; they cause each other, at least in part; they are both caused by a third factor, e.g. the number of people visiting the area; they are correlated by chance

5. Yes, it is incorrect – there is a fence post at either end of each panel and the post between two panels is shared, therefore, the number of posts is one greater than the number of panels

6. Any six numbers – as the system is designed to be completely unbiased, all numbers should come up with equal frequency and there is no 'more probable' choice

PRACTICE QUESTIONS (Page 47)

1. The multiplier that Julio has used is incorrect: 4% is 0.04 not 0.4 [1]; it is compound interest, not simple interest [1]; $1.04^5 \times 10\,000$ [1]; = £12 166.53 [1]

2. Emanuele has added 20% of the new price [1]; £75 represents 80% or $1 - 0.2$ [1]; $\frac{75}{(1 - 0.2)}$ [1]; = £93.75 [1] (Accept alternative methods of calculations, like those covered in Day 2 on pages 20–21)

3. There seem to be three students missing from the 30 (total frequency is 27) [1]; mean calculation needs to use mid-points of class intervals as a better estimate [1]; $(1 \times 5) + (3.5 \times 10) + (6.5 \times 9) + (9.5 \times 3) = 127$ [1]; $\frac{127}{27} = 4.70$ (no information on the missing three values, so use 27 for the calculation) [1]; median calculation needs to use values not frequencies [1]; the median value would be about 5 (the median value would be 14th value, i.e. the 9th value in the $2 \le n < 5$ class group, so $0.9 \times (5 - 2) + 2 = 4.7$) [1]

4. $2.75 \times 40 = 110$ [1]; but this is an *increase* of 175% not 275% [1]

5. The calculation is correct based on simple monthly interest [1]; simple interest: $\frac{6}{12} = 0.5\%$ per month, $\frac{1000 \times 0.5}{100} = £5$ [1]; for a compound interest rate: $1.06 = x^{12}$, $x = 1.00487$ [1]; he would earn £4.87 at the end of the month [1]

6. She has calculated 40% of the entire £42 385 [1]; she only needs to pay 40% tax on the amount above £42 385, i.e. £45 000 – £42 385 = £2615 [1]; $0.4 \times £2615 = £1046$ [1]; she pays 20% of tax on the amount between 10 600 and 42 385, i.e. £31 785 [1]; $0.2 \times £31\,785$ = £6357 [1]; this gives a total tax of £7403 [1]

Summarising and Writing Reports

QUICK TEST (Page 50)

1. Relevant, accurate information from a reliable source

2. Primary sources provide first-hand evidence (academic source); second sources report on primary sources (media)

3. **Any three from:** emotive comments; vague comments; contradictory comments; unjustified assumptions

4. It should be =(E1+E2+E3)/3 (BIDMAS)

5. Correlation does not imply causality, i.e. just because two values have a mathematical correlation does not mean one causes the other; there could, as in this case, be a third variable, e.g. weather, or some other explanation

6. Use of emotive language; lack of evidence that there is 'nothing wrong'; one example is not a general trend

7. It is very small sample of the whole population (Paris is not France)

8. The phrase 'might be' gives almost no validity to the statement

PRACTICE QUESTIONS (Page 51)

1. The total number of students is not 30 (it is 31) [1]; Marie only asked people in her class [1]; emotive language, i.e. 'a massively' [1]; the number of students who expressed an opinion was small compared to those with no opinion [1]

2. Asking only her year is not a good sample for all adolescents [1]; the information on other screens is irrelevant [1]; the column of data for TV does not add up to 90 [1]; there are no possibilities for 0 or more than 6 [1]; what does '2 hours' actually mean: 1.5 to 2.5 or 1 to 2? [1]; the calculation for mean is wrong – adding the values for TV and other screens will repeat some students and the other screen information is irrelevant [1]

3. There is no information about exactly when and where the survey was carried out – it could have been outside a cinema, which would have affected the results [1]; neither sample was statistically large, although the sample of men is twice as big as for women and might, therefore, be more accurate [1]; it looks like he should have used the title 'Mean' rather than 'Totals' [1]; the calculation for the mean value for each film, at the bottom of the columns, is not a weighted mean – it should be: $\left(\frac{80}{120}\right) \times 5.6 + \left(\frac{40}{120}\right) \times 6.2 = 5.8$ for *Star Wars* [1]; and, by the same calculation, 5.2 for *Me Before You* [1]; the comments on women's preferences are emotive and without evidence [1]; An improved report should specify time and location, e.g. a survey of people's opinions about two films was conducted in the shopping centre on Saturday afternoon with 80 men and 40 women [1]; and comment on what the data actually shows, e.g. The results showed a small preference for *Star Wars* in both groups, though women generally rated the films higher than the men [1]

Critical Analysis

QUICK TEST (Page 54)

1. Given that there are a large number of people tossing coins for a large number of years, even very unlikely events will happen at some point; he could have been using a biased coin (even, in an extreme case, a two-headed coin!)
2. How many people were in the trial?; How do owners know their cat preferred it?; Was this one group of 10 out of several/many groups? (Accept any other sensible question)
3. More accidents could be recorded for daylight because there are far more hours of daylight than of fog; it may be because people drive more carefully when the risk increases
4. No, other factors need to be considered, e.g. weather, day of the week, whether it is a holiday/local festival, whether the location will be the same, etc.
5. It assumes that the recent increase will continue at the same rate for 50 years; and that no measures will be put in place for removing the manure
6. The areas of the different logos need to be proportional (the size of the Cool Dawgs' logo is much bigger than Burger Street's, directly to the left of it, given the comparative sales – the height is four times greater, but the area is around 16 times greater)

PRACTICE QUESTIONS (Page 55)

1. a) The Green Party's lead over the nearest rival has increased by 55.6% [1]; but the overall percentage of the votes has decreased significantly, from 35.0% $\left(\frac{20.7}{59.1}\right)$ to 28.3% $\left(\frac{20.5}{72.8}\right)$ [1]; so it does not really suggest an endorsement of their policies [1]
   b) Although they had the biggest absolute increase [1]; a similar argument could be made for the Green Party, which more than doubled its number of votes [1]; whilst the National Party received a similar number of votes [1]
   c) The percentage of votes gained by the National Party in 2012 was $\frac{20.7}{59.1} = 35\%$ [1]; in 2016, it was $\frac{20.5}{72.8} = 28\%$ [1]; so there was a significant increase in the number of people voting against the government [1]

The Normal Distribution

QUICK TEST (Page 58)

1. Mean = mode = median; produces a 'bell' shaped curve that is symmetrical around the mean; total area under curve = 1; x–axis is an asymptote (curve approaches zero but never touches it)
2. Approximately 68% of data
3. μ
4. $z = \frac{z - \mu}{\sigma}$, where z is the standard score, Z is the real variable, μ is the mean and σ is the standard deviation
5. The table only contains the probabilities, up to and including, standard scores to the right of the mean (0); to obtain probabilities to the left of the mean, symmetry must be used
6. Reading from Table 1, the closest standard score to 1.9876 is 1.99, which gives a score of 0.97670 (97.67% of the data lies to the left of this)
7. $1 - 0.97670 = 0.0233$ (or 2.33%)
8. Reading from Table 2, a percentage of 0.63 gives a z score of 0.3319

PRACTICE QUESTIONS (Page 59)

1. a) Let Z = hourly pay, so Z_1 = £11.88 and Z_2 = £16.05
   $z_1 = \frac{11.88 - 14.42}{2.66} = -0.95488\ldots$ [1]; $z_2 = \frac{16.05 - 14.42}{2.66} = 0.612781\ldots$ [1];
   So, $P11.88 < z < 16.05) = P(-0.95488.. < z < 0.61278\ldots)$ [1];
   $= P(z < 0.612781\ldots) - [1 - P(z < 0.95488)]$
   $= P(z < 0.61) - (1 - P(z < 0.95))$ [1];
   $= 0.72907 - (1 - 0.82894)$ from the tables
   $= 0.72907 - 0.17106 = 0.558011$ [1];

So, approximately 56.6% or 57% of employees have wages between £11.88 and £16.05 an hour [1]
   b) Let W = minimum wage of highest 5%, so, 95% lie below this wage and z = 1.6449 from Table 2 [1]; $\frac{11.81 - 14.42}{2.66}$ = 1.6449 [1]; which gives W = 18.795… or £18.80, so the minimum wage of top 5% of salaries is about £18.80 per hour (to the nearest penny) [1]
2. Let μ mean height of men = 1778 mm and σ 101.6 mm [1]; so, $P(Z > 1981) = 1 - P(z < \frac{1981 - 1778}{101.6}) = 1 - P(z < 1.99803\ldots)$ – use $z < 2$ for Table 1 [1]; = $1 - 0.97725 = 0.02275$, so approximately 2.28%, just above 2 out of 100 or 228 out of every 10 000 [1]
3. Let Z = length of part
   a) 20.03 is 1 standard deviation below the mean; 20.07 is 1 standard deviation above the mean [1]; as about 68% lie within one standard deviation so answer is 68% or 0.68 [1]
   b) 20.06 is 0.5 standard deviations above the mean; 20.07 is 1 standard deviation above. $P(20.06 < Z < 20.07) = P(0.5 < z < 1)$ [1]; = $0.3413 - 0.1915 = 0.1498$, so the probability is 0.1498 [1]
   c) 20.01 is 2 standard deviations below the mean. $P(Z < 20.01) = P(z < -2) = 1 - P(z < 2) = 1 - 0.97725$ [1]; = 0.2275, so the probability is 0.0228 [1]
   d) 20.09 is 2 standard deviations above the mean, so the answer will be the same as for part c) [1]

Population and Sample

QUICK TEST (Page 62)

1. Sample mean = $\frac{\text{the sum of all sample data points}}{\text{total in sample}}$
2. All members of a specific item, group or set, e.g. all the people in the UK, all the members of a club, all the iPhones in the world, all the satellites every built
3. Use of a statistic within a sample to represent the population, e.g. quality control of a type of car may include looking at only $\frac{10}{20}$ cars and finding such statistics to represent the entire pool of cars
4. A population includes all members of a data set (e.g. members of a club); a sample only includes some of the population (e.g. the male members of the club)
5. If bias exists within a sample it may give a false impression of the overall characteristics of the population
6. Bias can be introduced when choosing the sample, by the questions asked, by the location and method of sampling – ultimately the survey should try to be as random as possible and proportionately representative
7. The larger the sample size, the more likely it is to be representative

PRACTICE QUESTIONS (Page 63)

1. a) Mean = $(\frac{210.39}{10})$ [1]; = 20.139 kg [1]
   b) $\frac{(19.758 \times 15) + 210.39}{25}$ [1]; = 19.9104 kg [1]
   c) 19.9104 kg, as it is for the largest sample size [1]
2. a) Let Z represent the distribution, then $Z \sim N(340, 3^2)$ [1]; $z = \frac{(330 - 340)}{3} = -3.333\ldots$ [1]; $P(z < -3.33) = 1 - P(z < 3.33\ldots)$ [1]; $z = 1 - 0.99957$ (using 3.33 exactly) [1]; = 0.00043 or 0.043 % [1]
   b) 0.043% means a potential 4 out of every 10 000 complaints [1]; this is low but could still mean a possible 430 complaints for every 1 million bottles consumed **OR** perhaps this is ok for a drinks bottle but less so for items such as a new drug or cars and safety [1] (accept any other sensible comments)

Confidence Intervals

QUICK TEST (Page 66)

1. The interval of a normal distribution (of a population) in which a statistic will lie

2. Normally the population mean (μ) is compared to the sample mean: $\bar{x} \sim N\left(\mu, \frac{\sigma^2}{n}\right)$, where μ is the population mean, σ is the population standard deviation and n is the number of data points in the sample

3. $\frac{\sigma}{\sqrt{n}}$

4. Any confidence interval can be used, but often 99%, 95% or 90% are used

5. $(\bar{x} - 1.64 \times \frac{\sigma}{\sqrt{n}}, \bar{x} + 1.64 \times \frac{\sigma}{\sqrt{n}})$

PRACTICE QUESTIONS (Page 67)

1. a) Interval $= \bar{x} \pm 2.576 \frac{\sigma}{\sqrt{n}} = 15.64 \pm 2.576 \times \frac{4.1}{\sqrt{32}}$ **[1]**; $= 15.64 \pm 1.867$ **[1]**; $= (13.773, 17.507)$ **[1]**

b) Population mean = 18.3 is outside the interval, so the belief is unjustified **[1]**

2. $\bar{x} = 181.8 \left(\frac{1818}{10}\right)$ and $\sigma = \sqrt{39}$ **[1]**; Interval (95%) $= 181.8 \pm 1.64 \frac{\sqrt{39}}{\sqrt{9}}$ **[1]**; $= 181.8 \pm 3.413932 = (178.39, 185.21)$ **[1]**; as the population mean for similar jars outside this interval **[1]**; it seems to suggest evidence that the director's claims are justifiable, based on this sample of ten jars (it would need further samples to be more confident of the claim) **[1]**

3. $\bar{x} = 6.9$, Interval (80%) $= \bar{x} = \pm 1.28 \frac{\sigma}{\sqrt{n}} = 6.9 \pm 1.28 \times \frac{4}{\sqrt{10}}$ **[1]**; $z = 6.9 \pm 1.619086$ **[1]**; $= (5.28, 8.52)$ **[1]**; this is the interval in which there is an 80% probability that it contains the population mean **[1]**

4. $\bar{x} = 80$ and $\sigma^2 = 29$, Interval (90%) $= 80 \pm 1.645 \times \frac{\sqrt{29}}{\sqrt{n}}$ **[1]**; using interval (77.71987, 82.80334): $80 + 1.645 \times \frac{\sqrt{29}}{\sqrt{n}} = 82.801334$ **[1]**; $1.645 \times \frac{\sqrt{29}}{\sqrt{n}} = 2.801334$, $\sqrt{n} = \frac{1.645 \times \sqrt{29}}{2.801334} = 3.162278$ **[1]**; $n = 10$ **[1]**

5. $\bar{x} = \frac{\Sigma x}{n} = \frac{10774}{100} = 107.74$ **[1]**; $s^2 = \frac{\Sigma x^2}{n-1} - x^{-2} = \frac{1736695}{99} - 107.74^2 = 5934.466$, so $s = 77.04$ **[1]**; Interval (99%) $= \bar{x} \pm 2.576 \frac{s}{\sqrt{n}} = 107.74 \pm 2.576 \times \frac{77.035}{\sqrt{100}}$ **[1]**; $= 107.74 \pm 19.844 = (87.896, 127.584)$ **[1]**

Correlation and Regression

QUICK TEST (Page 71)

1. r

2. $(\bar{x}, \bar{y})$, i.e. the mean of the x and y values

3. a represents the y-intercept (where the line meets the y-axis); it gives the value for y when $x = 0$; b is the gradient or the amount the y value increases for every unit increase in the x variable; a is the same as c in the straight line equation $y = mx + c$ and b is the same as m

4. $r = +1$ does mean that all the data points lie on a straight line and this usually refers to a direct relationship or causation but not always – the context is important

5. $y = 16 + (3.5 \times 5) = 33.5$

6. Divide all x values by 1000 but indicate this in brackets, e.g. x(thousand). Scaling does not affect correlation or regression

7. Generally not (this is called extrapolation); if the scores are very close to the data range, then the results may be valid but care is needed

8. a) $r = 0.51939388$; a positive but weak correlation
b) $y = 0.4875x + 41.42$
c) y-intercept is at 41.42, suggesting that if $x = 0$, $y = 41.42$; this may be sensible, but depends on the context

PRACTICE QUESTIONS (Page 72)

1. a) $r = 0.407$ **[1]**
b) The sample is too small **[1]**

2. a) Using a calculator: $r = -0.95287$ **[1]**; the equation of the regression line is $y = 2.6337 - 0.0401x$ **[2]** (1 mark for $a = 2.6337$; 1 mark for $b = -2.6337$)

b) r shows a very strong, negative correlation and the data points should be close to a straight line, suggesting that the higher the charge the less traffic there is **[1]**; $a = 2.6337$, suggesting around 2.6 million vehicles if there is no charge **[1]**; $b = -0.0401$ suggesting a reduction of 40 000 vehicles for every £1 added to the congestion charge **[1]**

3. a)

Distance (km)	0.4	0.8	0.9	1.4	1.8	2.3	2.3	3.2	3.4	4
Rent (£)	510	470	430	340	400	320	290	140	100	120

Using the table, the equation of regression line is $y = 555.23 - 118.65x$ **[3]** (1 mark for all correct data points in table; 1 mark for $a = 555.23$; 1 mark for $b = -118.65$ OR 3 marks for stating correct equation in full)

b) Regression line drawn showing correct use of mean (2.05 km, £312) **[1]**; correct amount of data points above and below line **[1]**; line meeting the y-axis at approx. 555 **[1]**

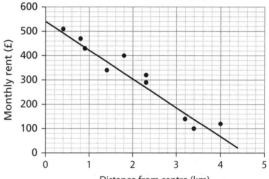

c) Using $y = 555.23 - 118.65x$ and $x = 3$ **[1]**; rent is £199.28, so £200 **[1]**

d) Any two from: mention of interpolation (within the data range) as acceptable and extrapolation (outside the data range) as generally not **[1]**; data points lie close to the regression line so reasonable to use for estimating **[1]**; reasonable to assume a strong correlation with rent being more expensive closer to the centre **[1]**; other variables such as proximity to transport, quality of accommodation, type of apartment (1, 2 or 3 bed/studio/local authority/penthouse) **[1]** (accept any other reasonable considerations)

Compound Projects

QUICK TEST (Page 75)

1. Which activity comes before (precedes) another

2. A diagram showing the different activities in a project and their relationships

3. Points in a network

4. Activity A, which has a duration of 1 unit of time (unit not defined)

5. Activities, predecessors and timings (durations)

6. Buy present (and paper, if necessary); cut paper to size; cover present; fold corners; tape paper (accept any other sensible sequence of activities)

PRACTICE QUESTIONS (Page 75)

1. Saving time, completing the project early **[1]**; saving money or receiving money earlier **[1]**

2. Not able to complete activities at the same time; might be a key worker on a critical activity, which would lead to delays (if no replacement is available) **[1]**

3. Predecessors listed **[2]**; and reasonable timings given **[2]** (1 mark for two sensible predecessors, 2 marks for more; 1 mark for 3 sensible timings, 2 marks for more; see example below)

Activity	Immediate Predecessor	Duration (mins)
A – Cook egg		5
B – Make toast		2
C – Butter toast	B	1
D – Cook beans		2
E - Put beans on toast	C	1
F - Put egg on toast	C	1
G - Serve	E, F	1

Critical Activities

QUICK TEST (Page 78)
1. a) The path through the network that will cause an overall delay if any of the activities on the path are delayed
b) The latest time an activity can be completed without causing an overall delay to the project
c) The earliest time that a particular activity can start
d) Float = latest time – earliest time – duration
2. Float = 7 – 4 – 2 = 1
3. If a critical activity overrun, the whole project will overrun/be delayed
4. Activities where the latest time – earliest start = duration (those with no float)
5. Working backwards from the end of the project; the latest finish time for an activity is the smallest number generated by finish time minus duration for all activities that follow directly on from it
6. R: 15 – 2 = 13; S: 17 – 5 = 12; latest finish time for Q = 12

PRACTICE QUESTIONS (Page 79)
1. a) A network with showing eight activities (A–H) **[1]**; with B and C shown in parallel **[1]**; and E, F and G shown in parallel **[1]**; an earliest start time of 0 for Activity A **[1]**; all earliest times correctly stated for B through to H (forward pass) **[1]**; a latest finish time for Activity H of 14 (weeks) **[1]**; and all latest finish times for Activities G back through to A correctly given (backwards pass) **[1]**

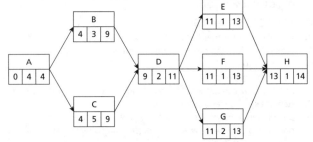

b) A, C, D, G, H **[1]**
c) 14 weeks **[1]**; this would give a finish date of 7 June **[1]**; but there are also two bank holidays and if it starts on a Monday, you would expect to finish on the Friday – 9th June. **[1]**
2. a) A network with showing nine activities (A–I) **[1]**; with D and E shown in parallel **[1]**; G and H shown in parallel **[1]**; and A shown with an arc directly to F **[1]**; all earliest times correctly stated for A through to I (forward pass) **[1]**; a latest finish time for I of 8 (days) **[1]**; and all latest finish times for Activities H back through to A given (backwards pass) **[1]**

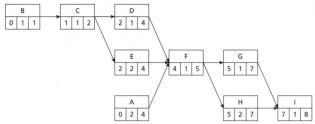

b) If B is delayed, the whole project will finish later **[1]**
c) E **[1]**; and H **[1]**; they are critical activities and have the longest duration at two days **[1]**
d) Critical activities E and H have been shortened by one day each **[1]**; the project should now take six days **[1]**; and finish at the end of Monday 8 July (if not working at weekends) **[1]**

Gantt Charts

QUICK TEST (Page 82)
1. A diagram showing all the activities in a project, with timings and sequences
2. The length of time required for an activity or project
3. The float
4. Concurrent activities are shown above or below each other
5. Time
6. A path through the diagram with no floats.
7. Planning and scheduling projects; assessing how long a project should take; determining the resources needed; planning the order in which to complete tasks; managing the dependencies between tasks

PRACTICE QUESTIONS (Page 82)
1. a) A Gantt chart showing nine activities with a total time of 8 days **[1]**; and the timings for each activity correctly plotted **[1]**; a float of 2 days for A **[1]**; and a float of 1 day for D **[1]**

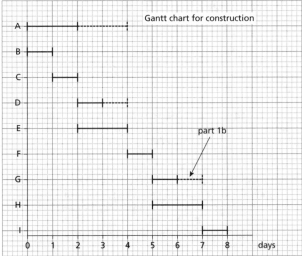

b) Latest finish time for G is now 7 **[1]**; so float = 7 – 5 – 1 **[1]**; float correctly added to Gantt chart **[1]**
c) C is a critical activity, so this will add two days **[1]**; G has a float of 1 day, so this will add 1 day, giving a total of 3 days **[1]**
2. a) A Gantt chart showing eight activities with a total time of 14 weeks **[1]**; timings for each activity correctly plotted **[1]**; and correct floats shown for B, E and F **[1]**

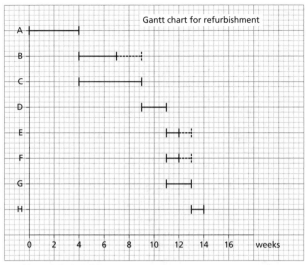

Gantt chart for refurbishment

b) A, C, D, G, H **[1]**

c) B has a float of two weeks, so no change **[1]**; D is a critical activity (+2 weeks) **[1]**; F has a float of 1 (+1 week) **[1]**; therefore, a 3-week delay and completion date 14 + 3 = 17 weeks from start **[1]**

d) From Week 9 until the finish at the beginning of Week 17, there would normally be 8 weeks of work, i.e. 40 days **[1]**; working 7 days a week would bring this to a finish in 6 weeks, i.e. by week 15 **[1]**; a delay of 1 week **[1]**

e) Five critical activities, therefore 5 weeks more **[1]**; so completed by Week 19 (18 weeks duration) **[1]**; should finish a week before Christmas **[1]**

Probability

QUICK TEST (Page 86)

1. The likely result based on probability and number of trials; expected outcome = probability × number of trials.
2. **a)** 2 red queens in 52 cards;
   b) There is now 1 red queen in 39 cards, therefore, the chance decreases
3. No, it is likely that one has a better record than the other
4. Strictly, no – not exactly; there is a very small, non-zero chance that the coin will land on its edge, so the probability is very slightly less than 50% (this is a bit of a trick question, but Level 3 Maths is all about thinking around the numbers)
5. Probably not – it is likely that the cars will be parked in the direction of travel on that side of the street
6. No, they are likely to be football fans and generally male (not representative of the population as a whole)
7. $0.65 \times 0.54 = 0.351$; about 35%.

PRACTICE QUESTIONS (Page 87)

1.

+	1	2	3	4	5	6
1	2	3	4	5	6	7
2	3	4	5	6	7	8
3	4	5	6	7	8	9
4	5	6	7	8	9	10
5	6	7	8	9	10	11
6	7	8	9	10	11	12

$P(\text{getting 5}) = \frac{4}{36}$ **[1]**; $P(\text{getting 8}) = \frac{5}{36}$ **[1]**; Gal should win $\frac{5}{4} = 1.25$ times more often **[1]**

2.

+	1	3	5	7	9
2	3	5	7	9	11
4	5	7	9	11	13
6	7	9	11	13	15
8	9	11	13	15	17

a) Zero, as an even number plus an odd number will always give an odd number **[1]**

b) 9 **[1]**; 11 **[1]** (see sample space above)

c) $2 \times 7 = 14$, 15 and 17 are more than double **[1]**; $P(17) = \frac{2}{20}$ **[1]**; $P(17) = \frac{1}{20}$ **[1]**; total $= \frac{2}{20} + \frac{1}{20} = \frac{3}{20}$ **[1]**

d) Yes **[1]**; there is chance of the score being less than 10 and a chance of the score being more than 10 **[1]**

3. **a)** $\frac{1}{37}$ or about 2.7% **[1]**

   b) $\frac{2}{38}$ or about 5.3% **[1]**

   c) The American system is much better for the casino **[1]**

4. The first card can be anything and the probability of getting the same kind of card on the next draw is now $\frac{3}{51}$ **[1]**; the probability of getting the same kind of card on the third draw is $\frac{2}{50}$ **[1]**, $\frac{3}{51} \times \frac{2}{50} = \frac{1}{425}$, so in effect the casino will pay out less than it gains **[1]**

Diagrammatic Representations

QUICK TEST (Page 90)

1. $\frac{8}{25}$ or 0.32
2. **a)** 16 (the value outside all three sets)
   b) It is likely that they would vote 'yes' at the referendum as 10 out of the 16% that voted for the National Party also voted 'yes' ($\frac{10}{16} = 0.625$)
3. $1 - 017 = 0.83$
4. **a)** 0.72
   b) $(0.72 \times 0.86) + (0.28 \times 0.77) = 0.835$
5. **a)** HT: $0.5 \times 0.5 = 0.25$, TH: $0.5 \times 0.5 = 0.25$; Total: $0.25 + 0.25 = 0.5$
   b) TT: $0.5 \times 0.5 = 0.25$

PRACTICE QUESTIONS (Page 91)

1. **a)** 15 + 3 **[1]**; = 18% **[1]**
   b) 2 **[1]**
   c) 16 + 15 + 1 + 5 **[1]**; = 37 **[1]**
2. **a)** A Venn diagram like the one below **[4]** (1 mark for each correctly placed value)

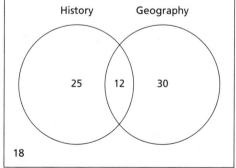

   b) $\frac{30}{85}$ or 0.35 **[1]**
3. Missing with first dart: $1 - 0.8 = 0.2$, missing with second dart: $1 - 0.75 = 0.25$ **[1]**; missing with both darts: 0.2×0.25 **[1]**; = 0.05 **[1]**

4. Correctly drawn sample space or tree diagram [1]; three out of eight combinations identified, i.e. HHT, HTH, THH [1]; probability of two heads = $\frac{3}{8}$ or 0.375 [1]

Combined Events

QUICK TEST (Page 94)

1. The probability of one event is not affected by another
2. Fair and independent, so 0.5
3. $1 - 0.27 = 0.73$
4. They are dependent, the probability changes, $P(B \mid A) \neq P(B)$
5. 0.5
6. $0.4 \times 0.6 = 0.24$
7. A or B

A or B

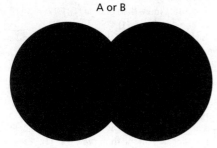

8. A and B

A or B

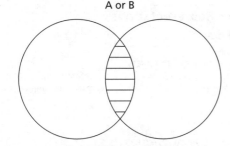

PRACTICE QUESTIONS (Page 95)

1. $\frac{1}{1000} + \frac{1}{120}$ [1]; $= \frac{1120}{120000} = \frac{7}{750}$ [1]; $1 - \frac{7}{750}$ [1]; $= \frac{743}{750}$ [1] (accept calculations using decimals to give an answer of 0.99)
2. The events are not independent [1]; as $0.28 \times 0.37 \neq 0.15$ [1]
3. The probability of not picking a blue sweet is or 0.47 [1]; so he is likely to lose his bet [1]
4. Start with 10 million people [1]; construct a tree diagram like the one below [1]; there are a total of 499 995 + 98 = 500 093 positive results of which only 98 are correct [1]; so, there probability that the person actually has the disease is $\frac{98}{500\,093} = 0.000196$ [1]; this is very small [1]; and a problem for the medical screening given the large number of false positives [1]

Medical screening

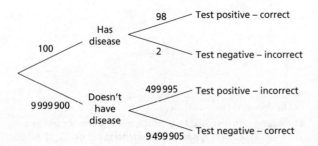

Expected Value

QUICK TEST (Page 97)

1. The expected loss would be $\frac{40}{36}$; he would make a loss of about 11p a go (based on the new pay outs (losses) being £3, £4, £5 and £6)
2. The 'average' (mean) value, given by the sum of the probability of something happening multiplied by its value, $p_1v_1 + p_2v_2 + \dots p_nv_n$
3. £20 fee; F: $(0.5 \times F) + (0.5 \times -10) = 5$, therefore F = 20; they could charge a promotional price of £20 and make an expected return of £5 per go
4. Expected daily cost: $(0.9 \times 0.1) + (0.1 \times 1.5) = 0.24$; for 220 days: $220 \times 0.24 = £52.80$
5. For 40 weeks of lessons: $(\frac{1}{8} \times 2) \times 40 = £10$

PRACTICE QUESTIONS (Page 97)

1. Probability of winning $\frac{1}{3} \times 0.2 = \frac{1}{15}$ [1]; expected return per week $= \frac{1}{15} \times 50$ [1]; $= \frac{50}{15}$ [1]; total expected winnings for 30 weeks $= \frac{50}{15} \times 30 = £100$ [1]; total paid for entry fees = $30 \times 5 = 150$ [1]; total loss = $100 - 150 = -£50$ [1]
2. The chance of it raining on any Friday is 0.3 [1]; the chance of rain on Saturday is 0.5 [1]; given that it rains on Saturday, the chance of rain on Sunday is again 0.5 [1]; so the chance of raining on both days is 0.25 [1]; the probability of a wet weekend is $0.3 \times 0.25 = 0.075$ [1]; there 52 weekends a year, so $0.075 \times 52 =$ about 4 [1]
3. Yes [1]; Consider a bet of y. Simone gains this y every time. If they throw a 1 or a 2 (a one in three chance), she will pay out $2y$. If they throw a 6 (a one in six chance), they need to get a 4, 5 or 6 (one in two) to win the $2y$. This gives an expected gain of: $y - \left[\left(\frac{1}{3}\right) 2y\right] - \left[\left(\frac{1}{6}\right)\left(\frac{1}{2}\right) 2y\right] = \frac{y}{6}$ [4] She should expect to make one-sixth of the money bet.

Living with Uncertainty and Risk Analysis

QUICK TEST (Page 100)

1. Cost without defences: $0.1 \times (1 \times 10^9) = £1 \times 10^8$; cost with defences: $\frac{2 \times 10^8}{20} + 0.01 \times (1 \times 10^9) = £2 \times 10^7$; therefore, better with defences by £10 million
2. The process of comparing the expected value of an outcome with or without the cost of a particular investment
3. Insurance companies work out the expected loss for an accident, etc., the costs of running the company and the desired profits and then charge this to the customers
4. Value of toaster: £45; likely to have a problem sometime in 5 years; cost of fixing problem £30, cost per year $\frac{30}{5} = £6$; administrative costs add another £4; so, £10 a year – probably not worth it for the customer
5. The question only contains information on loss, so comparing the expected losses: hundred year: $0.01 \times (5 \times 10^9) = £5 \times 10^7$; ten year: $0.1 \times (1 \times 10^8) = £1 \times 10^7$; all other things being equal, it would be better to protect again the greater loss associated with the 100-year event; this is, of course, likely to be more expensive and the council may not have the funds for this option
6. There will be some costs involved in starting up the business, i.e. materials, publicity, internet, social media presence, etc. and these may not be recovered if the business fails; the benefits include profit (if successful), employment, etc.
7. Estimating probabilities; assigning value to non-monetary items (what is the value of a sunny or cloudy day on holiday?); these calculations do not include environment, ethical, moral costs or benefits, etc.
8. Costs: initial costs (including research); capital costs for equipment; set-up costs; overheads; salaries; power, etc. Benefits: reduced costs; increase revenue; efficiency

PRACTICE QUESTIONS (Page 101)

1. Cost of toaster + expected cost of breakdown **[1]**; = 29.99 + (0.02 × 29.99) **[1]**; = £30.59 **[1]**; insurance would need to be less than 12p a year ($\frac{60}{5}$) to be worthwhile **[1]**

2. **a)** If there is a claim, the expected extra cost will be 0.1 × 500 = £50 **[1]**; but the saving will be 250 – 150 = £100 **[1]**; so it would be better to take the cheaper insurance **[1]**
   b) P × 500 = 250 – 150 **[1]**; P = 0.2 or 1 in five **[1]**

3. The expected cost of delays = 0.3 × 40 000 = £12 000 **[1]**; the cost of the cover is £10 000, which is cheaper, so they should rent the cover **[1]**

4. The expected value of an envelope = (0.25 × 1 + 0.25 × 10 + 0.25 × 100 + 0.25 × 1000) = £277.75 **[1]**; if they pay £50 only to find they have chosen the £1, the expected value of their opponents choice now increases to $\frac{1110}{3}$ = £370, an increase of more than their investment **[1]**; if they choose the £10, the expected value is now £367 **[1]**; if they choose the £100 the expected value is £337 **[1]**; if they choose the £1000, they just sit back and look smug **[1]**; no, it is not worth it – better to go second **[1]**

5. The probability × the value is the expected value **[1]**; recognise that this equates to the area under the PR curve, which looks like a triangle. **[1]**; Area = $\frac{1}{2}$ × 0.1 × 100 **[1]**; = £5 **[1]**

Control Measures

QUICK TEST (Page 102)

1. A way of reducing the probability of an event happening or eliminating it all together
2. Cost-benefit analysis
3. They might choose to maximise profit and ignore legal and ethical considerations (although this is illegal)
4. To reduce expected losses
5. 0.15 × 100 000 = £15 000
6. Advantages: save money; pay based on own driving skills rather than those of others
   Disadvantages: might not result in a reduction if driving is poor; there may be penalties for worse driving making it more expensive; privacy concerns

PRACTICE QUESTIONS (Page 103)

1. **a)** Approximately 100 days at 1 in 100 = 1 **[1]**; so each of the 5100 employs can expect to miss a day **[1]**; 5100 × 300 = £1 530 000 **[1]**; £1.5 million **[1]**
   b) Correctly drawn tree diagram (see below) **[1]**; cost of screening: 5100 × 10 = £51 000 **[1]**; cost of vaccination = (1530 + 340) × 5 = £9 350 **[1]**; cost of remaining staff being sick = (5100 – 1530) × 300 = £1 071 000 **[1]**; total = 1 071 000 + 51 000 + 9350 = £1 131 350 **[1]**; there is significant benefit to running the programme **[1]**

Screening and vaccination programme

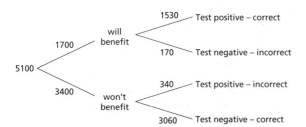

2. The idea that because all components are equally important the probabilities can be compared directly **[1]**; Part A: if the money were spent on A there would be a reduction every £10 000 by a factor of 0.9, so after £10 000 the risk would be 0.9 × 0.1 = 0.09 **[1]**; and with diminishing returns, a new risk of 0.9^{10} × 0.1 = 0.0349 **[1]**; an improvement of 0.1 – 0.0349 = 0.0651 **[1]**; If all the money were spent on B, there would be an improvement of 0.2 – 0.1 = 0.1 **[1]**; if all the money were spent on C there would be an improvement of 4 × 0.05 = 0.2 **[1]**; they should spend it on C **[1]**

3. Substance A: –5000 + (0.1 × 100 000) – (0.2 × 20 000) **[1]**; = £1000 **[1]**; Substance B: –3000 + (0.07 × 100 000) – (0.1 × 20 000) **[1]**; = £2000 **[1]**; assuming there is no additional loss of income associated with being caught or loss of reputation, if the athlete is concerned only with maximising their chances to make money, they should choose B **[1]** (however, as an ethical athlete, they should avoid making such immoral and illegal choices.)

Graphs of Functions

QUICK TEST (Page 107)

1. **a)** B
   b) E
   c) C
   d) D
   e) F
   f) A

2. **a)**

x	y
–5	–13
–4	–10
–3	–7
–2	–4
–1	–1
0	2
1	5
2	8
3	11
4	14
5	17

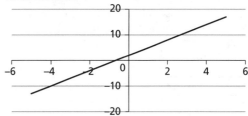

b)

x	y
–5	10.66666667
–4	9.333333333
–3	8
–2	6.666666667
–1	5.333333333
0	4
1	2.666666667
2	1.333333333
3	0
4	–1.333333333
5	–2.666666667

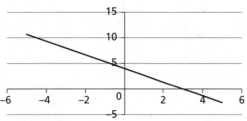

c)

x	y
−5	32
−4	21
−3	12
−2	5
−1	0
0	−3
1	−4
2	−3
3	0
4	5
5	12

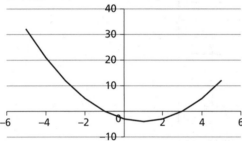

PRACTICE QUESTIONS (Page 107)

1. Correct table of values (see below) [1]; accurately plotted graph (see below) [1]; minimum point (4, 246) [1]; best radius is 4 cm [1]; as this requires the minimum amount of metal [1]

r	M
1	606
2	324
3	254
4	246
5	270
6	316
7	379.7142857
8	459
9	552.6666667
10	660

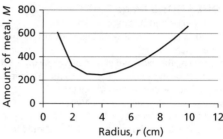

2. **a)** Cost on the y-axis and units on the x-axis [1]; correctly drawn line for Energy Less [1]; correctly drawn line for Wind and Gas [1]; correct intercept [1]

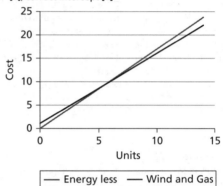

b) Wind and Gas [1]
3. **a)** Graph drawn showing height on the y-axis and distance on the x-axis [1]; correctly drawn line for Rocket 1 [1]; correctly drawn line for Rocket 2 [1]; correct intercept [1]; from the highest points on the two graphs, Rocket 2 goes higher by 50 m [1]
b) From the graphs, the first rocket goes 20 m further [1]

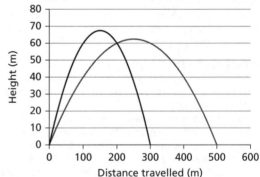

Intersection Points

QUICK TEST (Page 109)

1. No; for a sufficiently large order they would have to give the products away
2. Drawing a straight line between the points and extrapolating gives £42 (simultaneous equations would work too: $10a + b = 22$, $15a + b = 32$, therefore $a = 2$, $b = 2$, for 20 miles this gives £42)
3. As t is very large, the term $e^{-0.1t}$ will approach zero, therefore the maximum value is 9 volts (strictly never reached mathematically, but it will be for all practical purposes)
4. The rate of change will increase
5. On one side of the intersection, one particular company will be cheaper, on the other side, it will be the other company who is cheaper

PRACTICE QUESTIONS (Page 110)

1. An accurately plotted graph (see below) **[1]**; the line of best fit gives about £70 000 in 4 years **[1]**; so 2020 (another 16 years) would be an additional £280 000, giving a price of around £400 000 **[1]**; however, it is not likely to be a straightforward linear graph **[1]**; and the chosen period may not be representative of long-term trends **[1]**

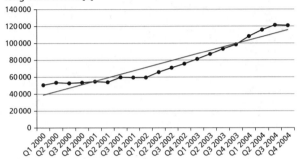

2. **a)** She can swim from about 12:00 **[1]**; to 16:00 **[1]**
   b) No, tide tables change throughout the year **[1]**; high tides are not always the same height/the time at which high tide occurs will change (depending on the position of the moon) **[1]**
3. **a)** The value of b is the value when $x = 0$ **[1]**; $b = 2$ **[1]**; $a = 0.5$ **[1]**; any correct method (graph, trial and error or algebraic) **[1]**
   b) At $v = 0.5$, $D = 2.125$ **[1]**; at $v = 10$, $D = 52$ **[1]**; any correct method (graph, trial and error or algebraic) **[1]**
   c) Most accurate at lower values **[1]**; as closer to the known range and the model may not be accurate for higher values **[1]**
4. At midday, the 20° elevation intercepts the line corresponding to a time in February just before March 1st **[1]**; and is more or less half way between October 1st and November 1st **[1]**; this gives approximately mid-October to mid-February **[1]**; a period of about 4 months **[1]**

Gradient

QUICK TEST (Page 114)

1. The gradient at a point on a curve, given by the gradient of the tangent to that point
2. **a)** £1, the amount the cost changes in relation to distance changing by 1 mile
   b) $C = M + 2.5$
3. At $x = 1$, $\frac{(2.25 - 0.25)}{(1.5 - 0.5)} = 2$ and at $x = 2$, $\frac{(6.25 - 2.25)}{2.5 - 1.5} = 4$
4. The rate will increase (this is an exponential growth)
5. When full, water will come out more quickly and the bucket will fill more quickly; the opposite is true when nearly empty
6. $y = mx + c$, where m is the gradient and c is the y-intercept
7. B (This could be illustrated on a graph. The intersection of the two lines shows the point in time when B becomes cheaper.)

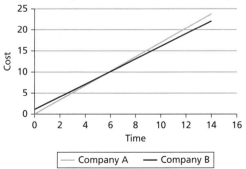

PRACTICE QUESTIONS (Page 115)

1. Correct table of values (see example below) **[1]**; accurately plotted graph (see below) **[1]**; gradient = 14 **[1]**; the point at which this is the gradient can be found graphically is $v = 20$ m/s **[1]**

Speed	Fuel Consumption	Gradient Line
0	0	−160
1	2.01	−146
2	4.08	−132
3	6.27	−118
4	8.64	−104
5	11.25	−90
6	14.16	−76
7	17.43	−62
8	21.12	-48
9	25.29	−34
10	30	−20
11	35.31	−6
12	41.28	8
13	47.97	22
14	55.44	36
15	63.75	50
16	72.96	64
17	83.13	78
18	94.32	92
19	106.59	106
20	120	120
21	134.61	134
22	150.48	148
39	671.19	386
40	720	400

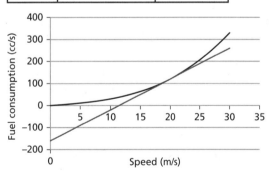

2. **a)** Day 4 (5 cm in one day) **[1]**
   b) Day 5 (2 cm) **[1]**
   c) 5 cm per day for 6 days **[1]**; = 30 cm **[1]**; starts at 5 cm, therefore 35 cm **[1]**
   d) Temperature, light, water or carbon dioxide concentration **[1]**
3. **a)** 06:19 **[1]** (accept answers between 6:10 and 6:30)
   b) Zero (maximum point) **[1]**
   c) Steepest part of the curve between 04:00 and 05:00 **[1]**; around 1.1 m/h **[1]**

Average Speed

QUICK TEST (Page 116)

1. $t = \frac{s}{v}$, $t = \frac{100}{70} = 1.43$ hours $= 1$ hour 25 minutes and 43 seconds
2. There may be sections of the journey where the car is travelling faster or slower
3. a) $\frac{70}{5} = 14$ lines
   b) 5 mph $= \frac{5 \times 1610}{60 \times 60} = 2.24$ m/s; distance in half a second is 1.12 m
4. $t = \frac{s}{v}$; Motorway: $t = \frac{65}{70} = 0.929$ h; A road: $t = \frac{65}{50} = 1.3$ h; time saved $= 1.3 - 0.929 = 0.371$ hours, equivalent to about 22 minutes

PRACTICE QUESTIONS (Page 117)

1. a) Inverness to Aviemore: 28 miles at 30 mph [1]; about 1 hour (with the time to leave his mother) [1]; Aviemore to Aberdeen, 63 miles at 50 mph gives, $\frac{63}{50} = 1$ hour 15 minutes [1]; Aberdeen to Inverness, 105 miles, $\frac{105}{70}$ gives 1 hour 30 minutes [1]; a total of 3 hours 45 minutes [1]; he has a total of 9 hours, so 5 hours 15 minutes for shopping [1]
   b) Total distance of $28 + 63 + 105 = 196$ miles, total time 3.75 hours (from part a) [1]; average speed $= \frac{196}{3.75} = 52$ mph [1]

Speed and Acceleration

QUICK TEST (Page 119)

1. Acceleration
2. Speed
3. The gradient (speed) is constant, which means that acceleration must be zero
4. Car A: $\frac{60}{5.4} = 11.1$; Car B: $\frac{50}{5.9} = 10.2$; Car A has the highest acceleration (units are not too important here as comparing like with like)

PRACTICE QUESTIONS (Page 119)

1. Assume the acceleration is constant [1]; the gradient at $t = 0$ is about 20, therefore 20 m/s [1]; the speed at about $t = 2$ seconds is zero (gradient horizontal) [1]; so, acceleration is about $\frac{(0-20)}{2}$ [1]; $= -10$ m/s^2 [1]
2. a) Athlete B [1]; they are moving faster at all times (the distance travelled is the area under the graph, so having a 'taller' graph means that the same area is produced at a smaller time value) [1]
   b) At the start the velocity increases from 0 to about 5 m/s in 1 second [1] so 5 m/s^2 [1]
   c) About 1 m/s^2 [1]
   d) Slows down [1]
3. A–B: constant speed [1]; $\frac{40}{20} = 2$ m/s [1]; B–C: stationary [1]; C–D: accelerating [1]; about $\frac{40}{60} = 0.67$ m/s^2 [1]; D–E: stationary [1]; E–F: return to origin [1]; at $\frac{150}{40} = 3.75$ m/s [1]

The Functions a^x and e^x

QUICK TEST (Page 124)

1. A function where the variable (argument) is the power of a constant, $y = a^x$
2. For example, $y = e^x$:

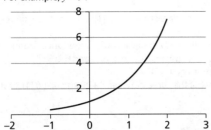

3. For example, $y = e^{-x}$:

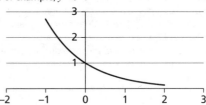

4. a) 15.6
   b) 1.44
   c) −2.06
   d) 0.0241
   e) 0.25
5. a) 8.17
   b) 1.49
   c) −1.68
   d) 0.302
   e) 0.607
6. a) $x = 5$
   b) $x = 1.666$
   c) $x = 1.532$ (3 dp)
   d) $x = -0.152$ (3 dp)
7. At $t = 0$, $N = 1$; when $N = 2$, $2 = 3.5^{0.7t}$; $t = \frac{(\log 2)}{(0.7 \times \log 3.5)} = 0.79$ hours, about $47\frac{1}{2}$ minutes (the time to double does not depend on the starting time – it will always double in size after $47\frac{1}{2}$ minutes)
8. For an exponential function, the rate of change (the gradient) is equal to the value of the function, so after 1 decade the value of the function (and hence the rate of change) would be e^1; this means that the amount is being multiplied by 2.72 every 10 years

PRACTICE QUESTIONS (Page 125)

1. a) 2500 [1]
   b) Sketch showing a graph the same shape as the one below [1]; starting at (0, 2500) [1]

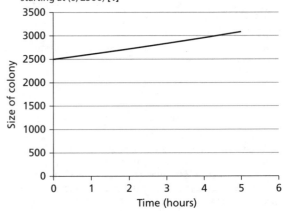

   c) 2836 [1]
   d) $5000 = 2500\,e^{0.042t}$, $2 = e^{0.042t}$ [1]; $\ln 2 = 0.042t$ [1]; $t = 16.5$ hours [1]
   e) No [1]; $2N = N\,e^{0.042t}$ [1]; $t = 16.5$ hours [1]

2. a) Yes [1]; 100, 68.5, 49.4, 37.9, 30.8 [1]
b) 20°C [1]; because this must be room temperature [1]
c) Sketch showing a graph the same shape as the one below [1]; starting at (0, 2500) [1]

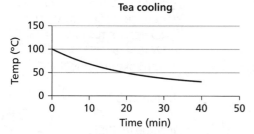

Tea cooling

d) Cooling quickest when $t = 0$ [1]; estimated from graph by drawing a suitable triangle (as shown in the graph) below and taking the fall as 40 degrees and the time taken as 10 min giving the gradient as $\frac{-40}{10}$ [1]; rate of change = -4 °C/min [1]

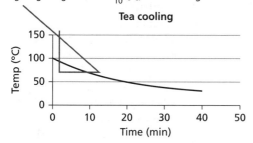

Tea cooling

Exponential Growth and Decay

QUICK TEST (Page 128)
1. 1.05
2. 2500
3. a) $M = 10\,000 \times 1.046^t$, where t is the time in years
b) $M = 10\,000 \times 1.046^5 = £12\,521.56$

4. Each 'level' is multiplying by five, so the number of people is 5^x, where x is the number of levels, $1\,000\,000 = 5^x$, $x = 8.58$, so nine levels
5. a) 8% less per year is 92% of the previous value, so a growth factor of 0.92;
$V = 3\,000\,000 \times 0.92^t$; $1\,500\,000 = 3\,000\,000 \times 0.92^t$; $0.5 = 0.92^t$; $t = 8.31$ years
b) At $t = 1$, $V = 3\,000\,000 \times 0.92^1 = 2\,760\,000$ and $3\,000\,000 \times 0.92^2 = 2\,539\,200$, loss = £220 800
6. Let m = number of months, then $\frac{1}{2} = x^m$, $\frac{1}{2} = x^{10}$, $\log \frac{1}{2} = 10 \log x$, $\log x = \frac{\log \frac{1}{2}}{10} = -0.03010299566398$, so $x = 10^{-0.030102...} = 0.93303299...$, so duration, $d = 0.933^m$, now $m = 24$, so $d = 0.933^{24} = 0.189$, 19% of the original

PRACTICE QUESTIONS (Page 129)
1. $600 = 1000 \times 0.9^t$ [1]; $0.6 = 0.9^t$ [1]; $\frac{\log(0.6)}{\log(0.9)} = t = 4.84$ years [1]; = 4 years 10 months and a few days [1]; so sometime in November 2021 [1]
2. a) 3 V [1]
b) V_0 is 3 V [1]; h is the time measured in half hours [1]
c) Assume 90% of the voltage corresponds to 90% of the full charge [1]; 90% is 2.7 V, $2.7 = 3(1 - 2^{-h})$ [1]; $0.9 = 1 - 2^{-h}$, $1 - 0.9 = 2^{-h}$ [1]; $\frac{-\log(0.1)}{\log(2)} = t$ [1]; $t = 3.32$ half hours, about 100 minutes [1]
3. a) $V = V_0 \times 1.048^t$ [1]; where V_0 is the initial investment [1]; and t is the time in years [1]
b) **Accept any two sensible assumptions, e.g.** compound interest [1]; that the average rate will be the future rate [1]; growth is a constant percentage [1]
c) $V = 25000 \times 1.048^t$, at $t = 3$, $V = 28775.56$ [1]; at $t = 4$, $V = 30156.79$ [1]; profit before tax = 1381.23 [1]; after tax at 45% = £759.68 [1]

Index

Acknowledgements

The authors and publisher are grateful to the copyright holders for permission to use quoted materials and images.

Cover & P1: Olexandr Taranukhin / Shutterstock; P5: Sascha Burkard / Shutterstock; P15 & P17: © University of Plymouth / cimt.org.uk; P23: stockyimages / Shutterstock; P24: Casper1774 Studio / Shutterstock; P27: wavebreakmedia / Shutterstock; P30: © economicshelp.org; P31: OBR / Open Government Licence P35: bunyarit / Shutterstock; P38: © Daily Mail; P39: Iain McGilivray / Shutterstock; P42: tylervigen.com / CC BY 4.0; P45: MSU/AMSU data are produced by Remote Sensing Systems / data available at www.remss.com/missions/amsu; P45: © NASA's Goddard Space Flight Center P49: doomu / Shutterstock; P54: pne / Pat Poseh / Mar1kOFF / folksterno / Tortuga / Shutterstock; P72, Q1: Marso / Shutterstock; P72, Q2: chrisdorney / Shutterstock; P98: Niyom Napalai / Shutterstock; P110: © Solentmet Support Group; P115: © Solentmet Support Group; P120: Gartner / Strategy Analytics

Every effort has been made to trace copyright holders and obtain their permission for the use of copyright material. The author and publisher will gladly receive information enabling them to rectify any error or omission in subsequent editions. All facts are correct at time of going to press.

Published by Letts Educational
An imprint of HarperCollinsPublishers
1 London Bridge Street
London SE1 9GF

ISBN: 9780008179724

First published 2017

10 9 8 7 6 5 4 3 2 1

British Library Cataloguing in Publication Data.
A CIP record of this book is available from the British Library.

Series Concept and Development: Emily Linnett and Katherine Wilkinson
Commissioning and Series Editor: Katherine Wilkinson
Authors: Jim Clayden and Simon Moroney
Project Manager: Rebecca Skinner
Project Editor: Rachel Allegro
Index: Lisa Footitt
Cover Design: Paul Oates
Inside Concept Design: Ian Wrigley and Paul Oates
Text Design, Layout and Artwork: QBS
Production: Natalia Rebow
Printed in Italy by Grafica Veneta SpA

MIX
Paper from
responsible sources

FSC
www.fsc.org
FSC™ C007454

This book is produced from independently certified FSC paper to ensure responsible forest management.

For more information visit:
www.harpercollins.co.uk/green